CW00853114

Victor
PUBLISHING
victorpublishing.co.uk

AFTER THE LORD MAYOR'S SHOW

MILLWALL FOOTBALL CLUB IN THE 1990s - Part One

MERV PAYNE

Victor
PUBLISHING
victorpublishing.co.uk

After the Lord Mayor's Show

MILLWALL FOOTBALL CLUB
IN THE 1990s - Part One

Merv Payne

First published in Great Britain in 2020

Published by Victor Publishing - victorpublishing.co.uk

ISBN: 9798621800918

Acknowledgements

◇◇◇◇◇◇◇◇◇◇◇◇◇◇◇◇◇◇◇◇◇◇◇◇◇◇◇◇◇◇◇

I would like to say a massive thank you to Ian Dawes for providing both the foreword to this book and for his many memories of playing for Millwall. I'd also like to thank Les Briley for his contributions.

Thanks also to Peter and Andrew Youngman for providing the fantastic images for the front cover of the book.

Contents

Foreword by Ian Dawes **3**
Introduction 11
Season 90-91 The Sheringham Show **17**
Chapter 1 Rioch-ing All Over the World 19
Chapter 2 Malcolm in the Middle 25
Chapter 3 Dropping the Ball 31
Chapter 4 Brighton Shock 51
Season 91-92 Millwall Mick **61**
Chapter 5 Life Without Teddy 63
Chapter 6 Keep Picking That Bogie 77
Chapter 7 Pompey Crimes 85
Chapter 8 Mick Caretaker 97
Season 92-93 Farewell Old Friend **105**
Chapter 9 The Final Countdown 107
Chapter 10 Lions' Feast - and Famine 125
Chapter 11 Den End Game 141
Season 93-94 A Rum Do **147**
Chapter 12 Culture Shock 149
Chapter 13 There's No Place Like Home 157
Chapter 14 Old Habits Die Hard 171
Chapter 15 It's The Hope That Kills You 187
Season 94-95 Andy May's Dad **199**
Chapter 16 The Calm After The Storm 201
Chapter 17 Drinking in the Last Chance Saloon 215
Chapter 18 End of Dawes 225
Chapter 19 Going Uwe The Top 239

foreword

by ian dawes

After The Lord Mayor's Show

Foreword
By Ian Dawes

◇◇◇◇◇◇◇◇◇◇◇◇◇◇◇◇◇◇◇◇◇◇◇◇◇◇◇◇◇◇

I signed for Millwall on the eve of the 1988-89 season. It happened very suddenly and in somewhat tragic circumstances. I'd been a regular at QPR since I turned pro in 1981, but the manager Jim Smith had signed one of his ex-players Mark Dennis in my position and it was clear that he was going to start the new season with him so I was in the reserves.

Millwall's pre-season wasn't going very well and they'd set up a match against QPR reserves at The Den a week or so before the start of the new season. I knew the Millwall assistant manager Frank McLintock from his days at QPR. During the match he was taking the mickey out of me a bit and I and was having a go back, just a bit of banter.

Unfortunately Millwall's left back Nicky Coleman suffered a really bad knee injury in the match which ruled him out of the season, and would eventually end his career. The next day back at QPR Jim Smith called me in to say that Millwall were interested in signing me.

The move appealed to me straight away because I had a young family and wanted to stay in London. Coventry had shown an interest in me and I went to speak to them but as I was driving up there I thought: "No, this is not for me!".

I signed for Millwall and it was a bit strange at first because they were playing a different way to how I had played at QPR.

I was used to playing the ball into midfield but I soon got used to passing to Teddy and Cas who were two of the best centre forwards you could have. The players at Millwall at that time were much better than people gave them credit for.

Everything was different at Millwall.

In my first training session I tried to get the ball off Terry Hurlock and he sent me flying. I was used to QPR where there would be less tackling in sessions.

For example, in our Friday sessions before a match at QPR we would do lighter sessions where there would be no big tackles so there were no injuries. At Millwall they tackled the same in training as if it was a match, whatever day it was!

Then of course there were the Millwall supporters.

I learned straight away that as long as you were trying your heart out, the fans were with you. They want to see you try, but they want to see good football too.

That first season was great, doing so well in the First Division, going top of the league by beating my old side QPR at The Den, fantastic memories, even though we tailed off a little bit towards the end.

I even have happy memories of the next one, even though we were relegated at the end of it. We were playing Charlton at home at the start of the season and were two nil down. We pulled it back to 2-1 and then in the last minute I scored the equaliser, I didn't even know what I was doing up there!

When Bruce Rioch came to the club I was really pleased at first because I thought his style of play would suit me but it turned out to be the worst time of my career. One day you would see him and say: "Morning boss", and he would totally blank you. The next day you'd think 'I won't bother' and he'd smile and say "Morning Ian." He was like a sergeant major. You couldn't wear jeans, had to wear a tie and be clean shaven. Discipline is OK, but you can have too much. My contract was up at the time and I was playing week to week but he refused to discuss a new deal for me.

One week when Colin Cooper was injured I knew I'd at least be in the squad, but he didn't say anything to me. The poor kit man nearly had a heart attack when I told him I hadn't brought my boots because I hadn't been told I was playing. He started panicking and I felt sorry for him so I admitted I had them in the car, but that's what it was like under Rioch. It was a shame because we were the best side in the league that season but for some reason we just didn't turn up for the play-off game at Brighton, I think nerves got the better of us and we really felt we should have gone up automatically.

The next season just things just got worse. Bruce decided to let the coach Steve Harrison go. If it wasn't for Steve Harrison I think we'd have lynched Rioch! Steve was a good coach, and a really funny fella and things would have gone downhill much earlier if it wasn't for him. We never found out exactly why he left but, whilst I never actually saw it with my own eyes, I can confirm that the stories about Steve, a wardrobe and a paper cup are true!

When Mick McCarthy took over he did a really good job, he played good football and there was never an issue with him being a player and then taking over as manager. When we moved to the new Den it was as weird for the players as it must have been for the fans. The atmosphere was a bit strange but it didn't take long to get into our stride and again we should have won promotion automatically that year but I think nerves got the better of us in the play-offs once more. I really enjoyed the days playing under Mick and the football we played with the likes of Alex Rae and Malcolm Allen.

My Millwall career ended almost as suddenly as it had begun, and almost in the same match. By the 94-95 season I was struggling with a knee injury and unable to train all the time. If I played on a Tuesday, I wouldn't be fit to play again on the Saturday.

The surgeon told me that there would be no more operations so I knew the end was coming. We had an FA Cup replay against Chelsea at Stamford Bridge and I really wanted to play. I started but even in the warm-up I could feel pain in my knee when I kicked the ball. I played well though and was subbed near the end of the match, hopeful that I'd be fit to play in the next round the following Saturday - against QPR. I was desperate to play. I decided that if I could manage it, that would be it, I'd retire. I liked the idea of going out playing for Millwall at QPR after my last game for QPR had been against Millwall at The Den, but it wasn't to be. My knee was still swollen and that was it. After seven years at Millwall, that memorable night at Chelsea was my last game for The Lions. Not a bad way to go out though!

I'll always have fond memories of my time at Millwall and still follow their results - as do my two children who are huge Lions fans.

It's still a very unique club, I hope it stays that way.

After The Lord Mayor's Show

After The Lord Mayor's Show

Introduction

◇◇◇◇◇◇◇◇◇◇◇◇◇◇◇◇◇◇◇◇◇◇◇◇◇◇◇◇◇◇◇

The summer of 1990 saw England simmering. Not just from a snap August heatwave that would cool as quickly as it had arrived, but from a social tension not seen in a decade. Its leader, the previously indomitable Margaret Thatcher, was starting to falter. People took to the streets and prisoners took to the roofs as the happy, loved-up glow that the country had been bathing in at the end of the eighties disappeared quicker than you could say "Poll Tax".

Thankfully we still had football.

Liverpool were champions again, claiming an 18th league title following their blip the previous season when Arsenal stole it from under their noses in the final moments of an Anfield thriller. No doubt normal business would be resumed, and the Merseyside machine would continue to dominate the 1990s as they had done the previous decade.

England's national team had once again played fast and lose with the nation's emotions, reaching a World Cup semi final for the first time since they won the trophy back in 1966, only to lose it on penalties to eventual winners West Germany. It would be the last time we'd called them that. The Berlin wall was about to come down and nothing would be quite the same again in Europe. Apart from them still beating us on penalties of course.

Leeds were back in the big time. Vinnie Jones inspired Howard Wilkinson's men to the Second Division title as they swapped places with Millwall who, after their two year adventure in the top flight for the first time in their history, were determined to reclaim that place at the first attempt and make the new decade even more memorable than the previous one.

It would be of course, but for entirely different reasons.

This is the story of Millwall Football Club's 1990s. A decade that saw them start in the top division, knock down their famous ground, almost go out of business and make their first trip to Wembley since the Wartime Cup Final defeat against Chelsea in 1945 which, given the amount of ringers featuring for each war-torn squad, didn't really count did it?

Millwall's brief stay in Division One saw them occupy just about every possible league position in the 20-team table. From the highs of hitting top spot in October 1988 and September 1989, to the final lows of being relegated in bottom place. Some of the leading names in reaching that pinnacle of the club's achievements had gone including striker Tony Cascarino and manager John Docherty – and another of the key protagonists would depart before the new season started too – but they still had Teddy Sheringham. For that particular young man, a very special decade was about to begin.

Millwall's board of directors quickly realised that the club was seriously boxing above its weight financially and set about altering that. But with an aging stadium that crumbled when they so much as nailed up a picture and needed thousands of pounds of maintenance work every six months just to remain standing, they were fighting a losing battle. Or to put it in the words of director Peter Mead: "It was like trying to put out a burning building with little plastic cups of water".

Midway through the club's second and final season in the First Division they announced plans to float the club on the stock exchange and by the time the new season had begun, Millwall FC were Millwall PLC and the only football club listed on the stock exchange outside England's top division. Further plans to invest in a chain of pubs were on the cards too and the elephant in the room – making the move away from The Den - was also well under way to being addressed.

As the nineties kicked in, life was moving fast and the game of football certainly wasn't standing still. After two years of ITV's big money television deal, the first signs of the rich getting richer and beginning to pull away from the rest were very clear. Manchester United, having survived a relegation scare and kept Alex Ferguson in a job by winning the FA Cup, would be one of England's first representatives in Europe after the ban following the Heysel Stadium riot was lifted. United's impatient fans were desperate to be at least challenging again for a league title that had eluded them for almost a quarter of a century.

In the Second Division there were some big names looking to get back into the top division. Recently relegated West Ham, Newcastle and Sheffield Wednesday's huge fanbases would not tolerate second rate football for long and there didn't really seem to be anyone to challenge them – certainly not financially – although up at

Blackburn, a certain Jack Walker was preparing to blow any other football club out of the water in terms of investment in a move that would change and shape the game forever.

Football had ambled along it seemed for the last thirty years. Very little changed throughout the sixties, seventies and most of the eighties. A walk down Cold Blow Lane and into The Den was much the same in 1989 as it was in 1969. But now the nineties were here. It was a decade that would change football and Millwall for good.

90/91

the sheringham show

1

Rioch-ing All Over The World

◇◇◇◇◇◇◇◇◇◇◇◇◇◇◇◇◇◇◇◇◇◇◇◇◇◇◇◇◇◇

The Football League fixture computer had provided Millwall with a gentle start to their Second Division campaign. A trip to Watford to play The Hornets for the first time in a decade, and then the old faithful opener at The Den: Barnsley. Just as it had been two seasons ago when Millwall embarked on that memorable history-making Second Division championship-winning season. Coincidentally, the last match of the season would be the same too: Blackburn at home. Superstitious Lions fans could only dream that the end result would also be the same.

All eyes were on two dates much later in the season though: November 10th and February 23rd - the two matches against old rivals West Ham. It wasn't really that much of a culture shock for Millwall fans, they had hardly become used to facing Liverpool, Arsenal, Manchester United,

Spurs and Everton on a regular basis anyway and neither of these season-opening matches were any more uninspiring than Coventry or Luton had become in a short space of time. It wouldn't be sour grapes to say that Division One had become quite boring in a surprisingly short space of time.

This was a fresh challenge. Fresher than ever. Probably for the first time ever, Millwall would be in a relatively high-profile position of being expected to challenge for promotion. The bookies never really gave The Lions a chance in their pre-season odds, but no-one could deny their promotion credentials with a strong squad of top-flight experience.

Only twice in the club's history had they managed to bounce back from relegation at the first attempt but aiming to leap back into Division One was a very different trick to try.

They would be doing it with a squad that might well have been good enough to keep them there had they been able to assemble it twelve months before. They would also be doing it with a new manager, a very different one to any Millwall Football Club had appointed before.

You'd have to go back to the seasons either side of the Second World War to find a time when Millwall chose a manager with any sort of reputation or track record in the game. The majority of their choices had either been recently retired players cutting their teeth on their first managerial appointment, or lower league jobbing bosses with a modicum of 'success on a shoestring' featuring most prominently on their CVs.

Bruce Rioch was a little different. Sure, he was still relatively new to the managerial game, but at the level Millwall were now competing, he probably had the best recent record having won promotion with Middlesbrough during Millwall's championship-winning season two years previously.

He was brought in to relieve Bob Pearson just in time for the final curtain call of The Lions' First Division adventure. The reaction of the Millwall fans to the news was largely favourable. The appointment of Rioch and his assistant Ian McNeil was made within 48 hours of the Good Friday defeat at Derby which confirmed Millwall's relegation, as they faced Tottenham at home.

After witnessing the 1-0 loss to Spurs following his appointment, he had three remaining matches to assess his new team. Routine defeats to Aston Villa and Arsenal away, and a final day loss at home to Chelsea produced four defeats, seven goals conceded and just a solitary, last kick goal in the dying minutes of Millwall's brief First Division lives scored by new signing Malcolm Allen who had provided one of the few bright moments at the tail end of a truly dreadful season.

In his fist ever programme notes, Rioch kept it safe and simple, making no promises about how quickly his goal of returning the club to the top-flight could be achieved. He highlighted what he saw as a bad imbalance in the team with only three left-footed players at the club -two of which were injured.

In all honestly, it was no more than they had been promoted with two years before, but Lions fans reading it might have been encouraged by him pointing out such details and the need to fix them – which would hopefully also mean more new players arriving.

Highly-respected fanzine The Lion Roars hailed Rioch's arrival as the signing of "a proper manager". That was in no way a slight against the brilliant Docherty, but a nod to the fact that Millwall had never before been able to bring in a manager with a proven track record at a higher level in the English league. It wasn't an appointment that was going to stop the presses or fill the back pages in the way a Brian Clough would have done obviously – but that was never likely to happen anyway, even though director Peter Mead wanted the board to go all out to try and tempt Cloughie to The Den.

Mead felt that if they offered him a bumper £250,000 per year salary he might be tempted to take the job and try for one last time to rekindle the magic that he wove at Derby and Nottingham Forest when he took both clubs from the Second Division to top flight and European success. The ambitious notion never received boardroom approval and Rioch was seen as a viable alternative.

It could be argued that Rioch was very much in the Cloughie mould. A strict disciplinarian who liked to play slick attractive football and a reputation for nurturing young talent and developing rough diamonds. A perfect fit for Millwall? Only time would tell.

Just two new additions were made to the squad before the start of the new season, both from north of the border. Midfielders Alex Rae and John McGlashan arrived from Falkirk and Montrose respectively.

It presented Rioch with something of an embarrassment of riches in the middle of the park, so something had to give, and when it did it shocked Lions fans to the core, coming completely out of the blue and on the eve of the new season. Making way in the Millwall midfield for the two new arrivals and moving in the opposite direction to join Scottish giants Rangers was none other than Terry Hurlock.

2

Malcolm in the Middle

◇◇◇◇◇◇◇◇◇◇◇◇◇◇◇◇◇◇◇◇◇◇◇◇◇◇◇◇◇◇

Millwall without Hurlock was almost unthinkable. In the last six months, three of the most notable characters in Millwall's history had departed the club: striker Tony Cascarino, manager John Docherty and now Terry Hurlock.

It was a stinging blow to Lions fans whose hopes of a genuine challenge for promotion had been buoyed by the club's resistance to allow any of its top players to be tempted to remain in Division One.

Whilst they still had Les Briley, Hurlock was a vital part of that spine of the team that included central defenders Alan McLeary and Steve Wood and striker Teddy Sheringham.

The news filtered around the away terrace at Watford as the teams warmed up for that first match of the season. Hurlock had completed his dream Ibrox move late on the Thursday night and, in this pre-Internet and social media era, many fans were still unaware of the deal being done.

It was a deal worth a reported £375,000. A fairly good bit of business in 1990, but at a time when transfer fees were just about beginning their steep upward trajectory, there's no doubt Millwall could have haggled for closer to half a million – and it's almost a certainty that, twelve months later, had he been part of another successful Millwall promotion campaign, his value would have eased into seven figures.

Thankfully, the three thousand or so travelling Lions fans that made the short trip around the M25 to Hertfordshire didn't have to dwell too much on whether or not they would miss Hurlock. New man Alex Rae enjoyed a solid debut and his bustling style, whilst not quite at the level of old Terry's, certainly showed encouraging signs of establishing him as another crowd favourite.

In between goading 19-year-old Watford debutant goalkeeper David James who was having a torrid time, Millwall fans had two Malcolm Allen goals to cheer in a far more convincing win than the final scoreline of 2-1 suggested.

Back at The Den on another scorching late summer day a week later it was Allen again amongst the goals and putting strike partner Teddy Sheringham in the shade against Barnsley. Rae further enhanced his early promise by grabbing his first goal for the club soon after to give Millwall a commanding first half lead and second half efforts from Jimmy Carter and then inevitably Sheringham added the gloss to a far more accurate 4-1 drubbing of the Yorkshire side.

Two wins from two bettered starts made even in Millwall's banner seasons of 87-88 and 88/89. It will never win you anything of course – other than perhaps the wildly optimistic notions of utter domination that every fan dreams of in a promotion season, but they would need to do it against far tougher opposition. That would come next with a trip to title favourites Newcastle.

From the first whistle, Millwall ripped into Newcastle with slick, decisive football that saw Sheringham, Carter and Allen torment them. Inevitably, it only took until the eleventh minute for that combination to give them a deserved lead.

Sheringham, with typical swagger, held the ball up just long enough for Carter to make another darting run behind The Magpies' left back. Carter's early first time ball was played flat and cut back to the edge of the six yard box instead of being crossed high into the danger area where

Malcolm Allen was lurking ready to pounce and slam a first time shot into the net.

Newcastle striker Mick Quinn was a constant threat but Millwall's defence looked as solid as it had done during the promotion run-in of 1988. Early in the second half a throw deep in the Newcastle half on the right was collected by Allen just inside the box. His attempt to turn the defender was blocked, but only as far as Carter who looped a deflected cross into the area just a yard from the line.

Les Briley's downward header was blocked by Burridge in the Newcastle goal but fell perfectly for Sheringham to tap home the second. Briley remained on the deck as Millwall's players and fans celebrated. The Lions skipper had been taken out completely by Burridge as he attempted to claim the cross but the eccentric stopper's efforts had only served to open up the entire goal for the lethal Sheringham.

With maximum points from the first three matches, one of Millwall's best ever starts to a season had seen them hit eight goals. Sheringham was looking more ruthless with every match and Alex Rae had been a revelation, bossing the midfield and giving defences headaches with his non-stop running. Jimmy Carter had clearly added not just a yard or two to his already lightning-quick pace but a First Division-tuned Rolls Royce engine to power it. The real standout performer though was Malcolm Allen.

With four of the those eight goals, he looked every bit the classy top flight striker that had performed so well in Norwich's title-challenging team of recent seasons and had Millwall fans scratching their heads at how they had been able to snare such a bargain.

Allen was so much more than goals. His pace and trickery dovetailed beautifully with Sheringham's intelligent hold-up play and defences were visibly panicked when faced with the three-pronged attack of Sheringham, Carter and Allen – with Rae marauding menacingly just behind.

Things were going far better than anyone could have planned. Had Bruce Rioch unwittingly unearthed the Millwall Dream Team?

Barclays League Division Two - September 8th 1990							
	P	**W**	**D**	**L**	**F**	**A**	**PTS**
1. Oldham	4	4	0	0	9	3	12
2. Sheffield W	3	3	0	0	8	1	9
3. MILLWALL	**3**	**3**	**0**	**0**	**8**	**3**	**9**
4. West Ham	4	2	2	0	4	2	8
5. Bristol City	3	2	1	0	6	3	7

After The Lord Mayor's Show

3

Dropping The Ball

◇◇◇◇◇◇◇◇◇◇◇◇◇◇◇◇◇◇◇◇◇◇◇◇◇◇◇◇◇◇

The top of the Division Two table as Millwall looked for a fourth straight win to start their season had a fairly unsurprising look about it with Sheffield Wednesday and West Ham occupying second and fourth places. Tucked in nicely in third were Millwall but out in front – albeit only by virtue of playing an extra match which they had won – were unfancied Oldham.

Millwall wouldn't have to face the unlikely league leaders until the end of the year, by which time it would be hoped they had exhausted their early season energies. Wednesday wouldn't visit The Den until the end of October and West Ham two weeks after that. With struggling winless second-bottom Hull and rock bottom Charlton next up for Millwall followed by mid-table Swindon, Portsmouth and West Brom, all The Lions had to do was keep scoring.

There didn't seem to be any problem with that when Alex Rae fired Millwall into a second minute lead against Ipswich but the expected slaughter did not materialise and suddenly Rioch was faced with his first managerial challenge of the season. Carter, Allen and Sheringham were snuffed out for the first time and as the game approached an edgy conclusion, Ipswich scored an inevitable late equaliser through Kiwomya.

There was a chance to get back to winning ways four days later with the visit of Hull and an early Sheringham goal looked like getting things back on track once more but again Millwall seemed to lose their way and in a shocking capitulation not only found themselves behind at the break but 3-1 down going into the last fifteen minutes. Thankfully a goal from Carter and a last gasp scrambled effort from Gary Waddock – in the for the injured Rae - salvaged a point but suddenly there were some worrying warning signs for Millwall fans to ponder over as they made the short trip to Charlton.

The first of three consecutive away matches saw the first of three consecutive goalless draws. Stalemate at Charlton was followed by another blank in the league cup first leg at Bournemouth and then another at Swindon. At Charlton, Rioch gave a first start of the season to young defender

Kenny Cunningham who had made his Lions debut earlier in the year and also a first bow for new recruit McGlashan. The two away draws were certainly no cause for concern for the still unbeaten Lions but the lack of goals and sudden loss of form of Malcolm Allen will have been.

Rae made a welcome return from injury and did so with another goal as the drought was ended with a 2-0 win at home against Portsmouth and there was more good news on the injury front with wingers Kevin O'Callaghan and Paul Stephenson close to being fit for first team action. With Jimmy Carter, they would provide strong supporting roles for what was about to become The Sheringham Show.

Another quickfire start at home to West Brom was this time capitalised on when Sheringham struck twice in the first seven minutes. After also netting for Albion with an own goal at the start of the second half, he completed his hat-trick on 57 minutes and Rae made it 4-1 sixty seconds later.

Sheringham was at it again scoring both in the 2-1 League Cup second leg win over Bournemouth – for whom Trevor Aylott scored a consolation. Aylott a ghost from the dim and distant Millwall past, a player signed by the hapless Peter Anderson in the summer of 1982 intended to bring similar striking power to The

Den that Sheringham was now displaying.

The first defeat of the season came somewhat inevitably away to Rioch's old side Middlesbrough. After receiving a hero's welcome back at Ayresome Park, Millwall then gifted the home side the lead with an own goal from Alex Rae before Hendrie extended the lead. Rae hit a late consolation but Millwall's unbeaten run had come away to Middlesbrough in October – just as it had during that first season in the First Division.

The recovery from that blip was instant, but all too brief. A brilliant team goal finished by Kevin O'Callaghan was enough to secure a 1-0 victory at Notts County who had edged above Millwall into fourth place before kick-off but defeat was again tasted – this time at home for the first time – when a first half lead was squandered to Bristol City. It wasn't the ideal preparation for the next big test: Ron Atkinson's second placed Sheffield Wednesday.

By half time Wednesday had silenced a shellshocked Den taking an easy 2-0 lead with David Hirst running amok and scoring both goals inside fifteen minutes, he almost completed a first half hat-trick but a smart save from Keith Branagan, in for the injured Horne, kept the score at two. Fearing the game would be out of reach before the break Millwall battened down the hatches and prayed for a second half miracle. It came of course in the shape of Mr Sheringham.

Jimmy Carter had pulled one back early in the second, getting on the end of a perfectly placed O'Callaghan free kick from the right-hand side. Before that two brilliant saves from Pressman in the Wednesday goal kept Millwall out in a frantic start to the second half. Sheringham's leveller was typical of the craft and skill he was now displaying.

He started the move with a ball over his head to the advancing Carter and was waiting on the penalty spot for the return pass to stroke it home. Sheringham was tormenting the Wednesday defence and came close to a winner on several occasions.

Just when it seemed they would have to settle for a draw Malcolm Allen made a welcome return to the goalscoring with a third in the final minute, finishing beautifully after picking up an O'Callaghan ball from the left, side-stepping a Wednesday defender and threading the ball into the net through the advancing Pressman's legs.

The Den was in pandemonium with scenes not witnessed since Neil Ruddock's last-minute equaliser silenced Brian Clough two years previously, but Millwall weren't done. Deep into injury time Sheringham had the ball out on the right hand side and sent in a lofted cross that was more like a deftly executed golf approach shot to the green from the rough. The ball seemed to hang in the air for an age, finally coming down just past Pressman's far post where Alex Rae had timed his run to perfection to gleefully nod into the bottom corner and send The Den wild once more.

In one of the most spectacular wins witnessed at The Den for many years, it should have provided the springboard for Millwall to go on and establish their place in the promotion places. What actually followed was a continuation of the club's often-repeated ritual of giving the better teams the game of their lives – and the struggling ones an easy ride.

Defeats to struggling Blackburn, Oxford and Plymouth sandwiched an impressive home draw in the long-awaited clash with West Ham where a crowd of over 20,000 saw Paul Stephenson give The Lions the lead early in the second half. Millwall dominated their second-placed opponents but could not add to their score and squandered two more precious points when McAvennie scored The Hammers' equaliser with fifteen to go. Meanwhile behind the scenes at The Den, almost fifteen years of speculation about the development of Millwall's home was about to be settled once and for all. Outline planning permission had been submitted to Lewisham Council and a survey of fans began. Unlike the previously doomed 'Superden' project which, in its various incarnations involved updating the current stadium, the intention now was to move altogether.

It was something that fans were understandably uneasy about - even though the new stadium would be no more than a goal kick away at nearby Senegal Fields. One thing was for sure though, this time the intentions were real and, as soon as Lewisham Council gave the green light the club would be on their way.

The findings of the Taylor Report after the Hillsborough disaster pointed to the need for all-seater stadia so a brand new build made far more sense, especially if it could be funded by the sale of the current land The Den stood on. The cost of bringing The Den up to the standards that would be recommended by the report would be impossible to meet.

There were a couple of departures that raised a few eyebrows among supporters. Youngsters Steve Torpey and Darren Treacy left for Bradford for a combined fee of £100,000. The Yorkshire club were now managed by for Lions' boss

John Docherty and he had already taken young defender Phil Babb to Valley Parade soon after taking the job and now added two more of what were considered promising young future Millwall stars. Such was the competition for places now though with the pressure on to go straight back up, their opportunities had been few and far between.

Also leaving was Wes Reid. The unlucky former Arsenal midfield man had been plagued by injuries since signing and his contract was cancelled after breaking down once more.

It was all change all round it seemed, outside of the football bubble, the country had a new Prime Minister. Margaret Thatcher had resigned as her cabinet revolted over European policy as the country slipped into recession. Britain's first lady PM had governed for eleven years, but the end when it came, was swift and 47-year-old John Major took over at number ten after a leadership election.

A goalless draw with Brighton which would haunt them much later in the season was followed by an unlucky League Cup exit 5-6 on penalties to Norwich but things appeared to hit an all-time slump in the run up to Christmas with a mind-numbing 2-0 submission at home to Watford and 4-1 humiliation at Wolves. The only saving grace was that Sheringham was still scoring, but the fact that he appeared to be the only player in any sort of form was a cause for grave concern as the year ended on a note of relief with a win at home to Leicester and the next one started with another – away to Port Vale. Sheringham was again on target in both and had now been joined by young striker Jon Goodman who had joined from non-league Bromley and marked his full debut with a goal at Vale Park.

More goals from Sheringham helped to make it three wins in a row as Barnsley were beaten away in the league and Leicester again defeated at The Den – this time in the FA Cup to set up another visit, and more fireworks from Sheffield Wednesday.

Absent from that cup win was winger Jimmy Carter. The reason given was an upset stomach, but the real one emerged less than a week later when it was announced almost completely out of the blue that Carter had completed an £800,000 move to Liverpool. Carter had been a huge part of Millwall's success that season and the provider of many of Teddy Sheringham's goals. The shock move had Lions fans wondering if it might have spelled the end of their promotion hopes. Those fears were settled a little with a 2-1 away win over top seven rivals Barnsley 48 hours after

Carter's move to Anfield with Sheringham on the scoresheet. By now Sheringham's bountiful season in front of goal had taken him beyond club record goalscorer Derek Possee.

Before the FA Cup fourth round clash with Ron Atkinson's men Millwall managed to shoot themselves in the foot once again though with a timid 1-0 home defeat to Newcastle who had failed to live up to their promotion-challenging billing and were languishing in fifteenth place. The FA Cup was a great distraction but Millwall fans were beginning to feel that, come the end of the season, they'd rue so many points thrown away against weak opposition in what was shaping up to be one of the most open Second Division promotion races in recent years.

What was to make it even more open was the fact that four teams would be promoted this season. With the Football League favouring a return to a 22-club top-flight, two would come down from the First Division and the top three in Division Two would be promoted automatically. The play-offs would be contested between the teams in fourth to seventh place, making this a unique opportunity for Millwall to regain that precious place in Division One. Whilst nobody knew it yet, now would be the perfect time to secure that place, and the worst possible time to miss out on it. Off the pitch, Millwall were making preparations to be in much better shape to make the most of top flight football should they be able to win promotion.

The programme for the Newcastle match revealed for the first time more detailed plans about the move to Senegal Fields following a fan meeting which was attended by several hundred supporters.

It confirmed that the outcome of The Taylor Report would recommend that teams in the top two divisions have all-seater stadiums and that to make The Den all-seater would cost way outside the club's means and reduce the capacity to a meagre 13,000.

It also confirmed that the new stadium - a model of which was shown in the programme - would be part funded by the sale of the land The Den was on and grants. The aim was to be playing in it by the start of the 93/94 season with Lewisham's planning permission decision imminent. After years of stalling, things were now moving quickly and Millwall fans would soon have to accept the sad reality of leaving their beloved home.

When Paul Stephenson fired Millwall into a first minute lead in their FA Cup fourth round tie against Sheffield Wednesday, fans just knew they were in for another footballing feast.

Goals from Hirst again and Trevor Francis put Wednesday ahead but Alex Rae equalised just before half time only for Pearson to make it 3-2 to the Yorkshiremen ten minutes after the break.

Sheringham levelled it up yet again with twenty minutes to go but it looked like Wednesday would have the final word when Anderson made it 4-3 with just five minutes left, only for Rae to grab his second in the final minute to leave Lions fans breathless once again. The sides couldn't repeat the magic in the replay which saw Wednesday record a routine 2-0 win and end Millwall's FA Cup for another season.

Now happy to concentrate on the league, Millwall went into overdrive powering to a 3-0 win away to Ipswich and blowing hapless strugglers Plymouth out of the water with a crushing 4-1 win at The Den - which saw Sheringham grab all four to add to his strike at Portman Road and set The Lions up nicely for the promotion clash at West Ham.

With Millwall now down to seventh they desperately needed to get something from the table-topping Hammers. After falling behind to a McAvennie goal in the seventeenth minute, Jon Goodman gave them hope with an equaliser on the stroke of half time but it was that man McAvennie again who did the damage restoring his side's lead in the second half and a Morley goal saw the game end 3-1 to West Ham.

A drab 0-0 draw in shocking conditions away to struggling Oxford was followed by a catastrophic late loss at Bristol Rovers and Millwall's split personality was starting to rear its ugly head once more.

There was no middle ground, they were either brilliant or awful and had now plummeted to ninth place with promotion seemingly out of the question.

Seventh placed Brighton were easily disposed of 3-0 at The Den next - another score which would resonate that summer - and four more useful points were picked up with a draw at Portsmouth and victory over Swindon.

Things were looking really bright when fourth placed Middlesbrough visited after goals from Thompson and Goodman put them two ahead in the first twenty minutes.

But they inexplicably let the lead slip in the final twenty and two more priceless points were thrown away. Millwall were dropping the ball once more it seemed, just when a place in those all-important top three automatic promotion places was within easy reach.

Meanwhile the club announced that their plans for a new stadium had been given the go ahead by

Lewisham Council and, subject to the formalities of being rubber-stamped by Secretary of State for the Environment Michael Heseltine, Millwall would play for just two more seasons at The Den before moving to their shiny new, purpose-built, all-seater stadium in 1993.

Three wins on the spin sent them up to fourth however and they took a useful point off of new league leaders Oldham who still hadn't faded after their early season form. Sheringham then gave another masterclass with his third hat-trick of the season in the 3-1 Den victory over Charlton. The problem was, if Sheringham didn't score, Millwall struggled, and in the three matches that followed they well and truly shot themselves in the foot. In an attempt to address this Rioch made two transfer deadline signings, one would be an almost instant success, the other a complete non-starter.

Paul Kerr had often been a major thorn in Millwall's side when playing against them for Middlesbrough - never more so than in that frustrating Den draw recently when The Lions surrendered the points.

So fans were pleasantly surprised when Millwall announced that the attacking midfielder had signed and teamed up once more with Rioch. The other new addition was veteran Mike Fillery who joined on loan from promotion-chasing rivals Oldham but the 30-year-old former Chelsea, QPR and Portsmouth midfielder lasted just 55 minutes of his debut in the 1-0 away win at West Brom.

In a bizarre coincidence, the last time this happened was back in 1986 when then Millwall boss John Docherty signed Gillingham winger Terry Cochrane on a temporary deal. He made his debut in a 1-0 win away to West Brom where Teddy Sheringham scored the only goal. Fast forward to 1991 where Fillery made his one and only Millwall appearance at the same venue, with the same result and, you guessed it, Sheringham scoring the winner again. Neither Cochrane or Fillery kicked a ball for Millwall again.

At the other end of the footballing food chain, Millwall's youth team were recreating a bit of club history. Tom Whalley's youngsters were enjoying a season similar to David Payne's all-conquering squad of 1979 with impressive displays in the South East Counties League, Southern Junior Floodlit Cup and the FA Youth Cup. Having reached the Southern Junior Floodlit Cup final to face Arsenal, they had been drawn against West Ham in the FA Youth Cup semi-finals and pulled off a stunning 2-1 first leg win at Upton Park thanks to two goals from Sean Devine.

Paul Kerr added some much-needed energy to the side but understandably would take time to settle in and once again teams struggling at the other end of the table proved to be Millwall's downfall. Port Vale arrived at The Den just above the relegation places and despite Dave Thompson quickly wiping out Vale's first half opener, disaster struck when Beckford grabbed a last minute winner for the visitors.

A trip to rock bottom Hull wasn't much better and the only consolation for a 1-1 draw was Kerr's first goal for the club.

Part of the problem for Millwall's stop-start promotion tilt was the unexpected challenge from unfancied teams. Oldham and Notts County had continued strong starts to the season.

Joe Royle's second placed Latics had now opened up a nine point lead over Millwall in fourth, with West Ham top a further three ahead of Oldham.

Sheffield Wednesday occupied that third and final automatic spot, four points clear of The Lions but with two games in hand.

Notts County had been lurking around the play-off spots all season and were five behind Millwall in seventh - also with two games in hand - so their visit to The Den in the penultimate home match of the season was huge.

County arrived brilliantly drilled by manager Neil Warnock and left The Den with all three points in a thoroughly clinical display, winning 2-1. Another goal for Kerr was scant consolation for a second home defeat in a row and the chance of automatic promotion was now virtually gone.

Meanwhile the youth team had completed the job over West Ham in the FA Youth Cup, winning 2-0 in the second leg at The Den to seal an impressive 4-1 aggregate win and a final place against Sheffield Wednesday.

It would be the first time that the final had been contested by two teams outside the top flight and a chance for Millwall's young lions to emulate the class of '79 who had won the competition for the first time in the club's history twelve years before.

The fans that travelled to Bristol City must have been both delighted and frustrated in equal measure a week later.

Sheringham was on fire, hitting his fourth hat-trick of the season in twenty frantic second half minutes.

Thompson scored the other in an impressive 4-1 demolition against a side looking to grab one of the last play-off places and it at least offered hope that, with Sheringham's goals, winning the play-offs was a realistic target - if Millwall could just find some consistency over three games!

Those Sheringham strikes at Bristol City took him over the 30 league goal mark and his 32nd came in the 90th minute at Hillsborough, but by then Sheffield Wednesday were ready to celebrate promotion having scored twice earlier in the game to seal that third and final automatic promotion place.

All Millwall could do was try and hold on to fifth place by beating Blackburn at The Den in the final league match. Three days before that 2-1 defeat to Wednesday, Millwall's youth team travelled to Hillsborough to play the first leg of the FA Youth Cup final and put on a stunning display to win 3-0. Six days later they completed the job at The Den to secure the trophy. Millwall became only the second team outside the top division to win the competition twice, matching Crystal Palace who had won back to back titles in 1977 and 1978.

Tom Whalley's young Lions were unable to make it a cup double after losing to Arsenal in the Southern Junior Floodlit Cup final but the FA Youth Cup was the one they all wanted. The club and fans could only hope that more was made of this latest talented crop of youngsters than their 1979 predecessors, many of whom made it into the first team but were sold off to ease the club's financial woes.

Notts County had secured the top play-off place

which would see them face the team qualifying in seventh with home advantage in the second leg. Neil Warnock's impressive side's late surge almost saw them pip Wednesday to the final automatic spot with seven wins on the spin - including a final day victory over promoted West Ham which denied The Hammers the title. In fact, had they managed to hold Sheffield Wednesday to a draw in their home fixture just before that run began instead of slipping to a 2-0 defeat, third spot would have been theirs. As it was, they were certainly going into the play-offs as the form team.

Sheringham equalled Richard Parker's 38 goals in all competitions record that had stood since 1927 with a penalty in the 2-1 win against Blackburn and results elsewhere saw Oldham lift the Second Division title trophy by a point over West Ham and Middlesbrough pip Barnsley to that final play-off place on goal difference to earn a daunting tie with in-form Notts County.

Brighton's 2-1 victory over Ipswich saw them finish sixth and they would be Millwall's first ever play-off opposition. For the first time Wembley awaited the winners of each semi-final, but for Millwall now there was far more at stake than just a day out at the twin towers and a place back in Division One.

Sheringham's goals had understandably attracted attention. Whatever Millwall's play-off fate was destined to be, he would almost certainly be a First Division striker come August.

4

Brighton Shock

◇◇◇◇◇◇◇◇◇◇◇◇◇◇◇◇◇◇◇◇◇◇◇◇◇◇◇◇◇◇

What makes football so unique and popular is that it is never an exact science. In many sports there will of course always be shocks and odds upset, but it's much more of a rarity in say rugby or cricket for example. More often than not in those sports, the better team wins.

Millwall travelled to Brighton for their first ever play-off match with the league results between the two hugely in their favour. In fact Brighton hadn't even managed to score against The Lions. The two teams battled out a goalless draw at The Goldstone ground back in November and Millwall swept them aside 3-0 at The Den in the return game.

Brighton had spent the first half of the season in mid-table and it was only two purple patches of five consecutive wins at the start of the new year and a four win run in March that had seen them sneak into a play-off berth.

Such was the magic of this relatively new end-of-season extension. The previous four seasons they had been played had produced knife-edge suspense to both the final matches of the regular season and of course the play-off games themselves.

Form going into them was crucial - and that was where Millwall and Brighton seemed well matched. Both teams had been awful!

Since that four match winning run for Barry Lloyd's Brighton in March they had managed just three wins and a draw in the final ten matches. Six defeats in your last ten games is almost relegation form, but Millwall hadn't fared much better.

They had managed to win half of their final ten, but three defeats in the last six was similarly poor. Lions fans that decided to pass the days leading up to that semi-final first leg torturing themselves playing that age-old football fan's pastime of "what might have been" will have seen some grim reading.

Usually Millwall's home form was the foundation of any successful season. A fifth place finish and play-off place secured had to be seen as a success but their return of just eleven home wins was the worst of the top nine teams and even equalled by mid-table Wolves and Bristol Rovers. Thirty points had been squandered at The Den with six draws and six defeats. Had they been able to salvage just a third of those they would have been celebrating promotion again.

An eight game winless run following that fantastic 4-2 home victory over Sheffield Wednesday also put paid to any hopes Millwall might have had of a golden opportunity of securing promotion back to the First Division. There was no point in going over old ground now though. Rioch's men had just over a week to prepare for the first leg at Brighton, secure their fans a first post-war Wembley trip and a place back in the top flight.

When Paul Stephenson swept Millwall into an 15th-minute lead from 25 yards at the Goldstone Ground, The Lions' travelling army of fans would have been forgiven for booking their places at Wembley on June 2nd. Millwall had dominated from the kick-off - just as they had in the 3-0 league win at The Den - and a similar scoreline looked on the cards. It was, but not how Millwall's celebrating fans imagined.

It all started to go horribly wrong when Brighton goalkeeper Perry Digweed launched a booming kick in the 40th minute after yet another Millwall attack. With Lions players furiously backpedaling, Millwall defender Dave Thompson had his back to the ball as it dropped centrally on the edge of the penalty area. Had he been able to evade the ball as he clearly tried to, it would have dropped harmlessly into the waiting arms of his 'keeper Brian Horne.

Instead it struck him on the back of the head and dropped into the path of the on-rushing Mark Barham who caught it perfectly first time to prod it home for the equaliser.

The circumstances in which the leveller had come clearly knocked Millwall. Instead of going into the break buoyed by what should have been a two or three goal advantage they had been pegged back by a freak goal. Now was not the time for the bad side of Millwall's Jeckyll and Hyde season to appear, but it did, and in crushing style. The second half began with Brighton clearly feeling the game was there for the taking and a still shellshocked Lions defence became virtual spectators as Mike Small and then veteran Clive Walker were allowed to storm through almost unchallenged in the 53rd and 54th minutes.

At 1-3 there was still a way back for Millwall and one goal would be enough to send them back to The Den with the confidence to save the tie. On the hour mark though Robert Codnor - a player who Millwall had apparently been interested in signing from Barnet - virtually ended the tie with almost two hours to spare. The goal was typical of Millwall's day - and season in many ways. On the attack, desperate for that vital goal back, Briley's pass out to Stephenson on the left was easily intercepted by Chivers and quickly played forward. Once again all of Millwall's defenders seemed to be committed forward as Small laid the ball off to Codner powering through the middle and, with acres of space, he was able to easily pick his spot past a hapless Horne.

The only saving grace was that Brighton didn't further add to the score but it didn't matter. Even the most optimistic of Lions fans didn't believe they could overturn a three goal deficit - even at The Den.

The truth was of course that, if they could just repeat that 3-0 league scoreline it would be enough to get them right back in it but in totally different circumstances and a world of new pressure, it was highly unlikely that Brighton wold allow this to slip. They had the firepower of course in 38-goal Sheringham, but he had been worryingly quiet in the first leg. It was in stark contrast to the speculation surrounding him though which was now louder than ever.

The First Division season had of course long since finished and the final act - the FA Cup final - played out 24 hours before Millwall's Brighton nightmare. Now, with thoughts firmly on preparations for next season, defeated finalist Brian Clough was on the lookout for reinforcements for his Nottingham Forest team. Rumour was rife all around the day of the Wembley showpiece that the deal for Sheringham had been done. It can't have been the ideal preparation for Bruce Rioch.

Millwall had to soldier on and pray for a miracle.

The Den was bathed in early summer evening sunshine three days later as it hosted its final match of the season. If Millwall were to pull off the miracle and extend that by one more at Wembley eleven days later, they would at the very least have to score early.

Rioch shuffled his pack and brought in striker John McGinlay to replace Goodman alongside Sheringham. John McGlashan made a rare appearance replacing Waddock in what looked like an attempt to shore up the Lions that had looked so leaky and vulnerable in the first leg when chasing the game.

The game got off to an understandably cagey start but burst into life after fifteen minutes. Paul Stephenson collected a ball from McGinlay just inside the Brighton half and sent a cross into the Brighton penalty area from the left.

McGlashan and Sheringham were being tightly marshalled by the Brighton defence close to the penalty spot and McGlashan's leap was only enough to get a glancing header on the ball and divert it frustratingly away from Sheringham.

However McGinlay had continued his run and arrived just inside the box completed unmarked. Taking time to control the ball and compose himself, he then slammed it past Digweed to spark pandemonium on the terraces and give Millwall the slimmest of hopes. What they needed now was another one quickly to try and inflict the same sudden shock tactics on Brighton as they had used three days earlier in the first leg - and it came.

Brighton immediately lost possession from the restart and another Stephenson left-wing run was diverted out for a corner. The kick was sent high over Brighton's far post where Dave Thompson was waiting and managed to bundle the ball over the line.

The ground erupted again as the realisation spread that the score was now just 3-4 instead of 1-4 and with more than three quarters of the game still to go Millwall would surely go on to win. Then silence. Referee John Martin - often a thorn in Millwall's side - had spotted an infringement amongst the chaos that had led to

Thompson's goal and chalked it off.

With that crushing blow the energy seemed to be instantly sapped from both Millwall players and fans. The momentum was lost and, as had happened in the first leg, handed over to Brighton. Within sixty seconds of the restart Codnor scored and Robinson sealed a devastating 6-2 aggregate defeat in the 70th minute. Millwall's season was over.

In truth it had been over as soon as Brighton scored their fourth in the first leg, yet for a brief few seconds when Millwall thought they had a second on the night, there was a glimmer of hope.

The two legs had perfectly encapsulated Millwall season as a whole. Brilliant in some spells, terrible in others. Millwall had one of their largest and most experienced squads in the club's history.

History would show that, in Sheringham and McGinlay, they also had two of the most prolific goalscorers in football league history, but both would go on to score the majority of their goals away from Millwall.

Injuries and inexplicable loss of form had deprived Rioch of key players such as Kevin O'Callaghan and Malcolm Allen. The size of the squad may well have proved to be hindrance rather than a help with so many different permutations of players used.

Notts County went on to beat Middlesbrough over two legs in their semi final and then Brighton 3-1 in the final. It was a fair conclusion for the side that had been the most impressive and consistent outside of the top three that season.

Elsewhere in the league, George Graham steered his Arsenal side to their second title in three seasons, finishing the season with just one defeat. Manchester United's revival under Fergie continued as they won the European Cup Winners Cup by defeating Barcelona 2-1. Derby and Sunderland were relegated from the top flight.

Eleven days after the final, First Division clubs informed the management committee of the Football League that they intended to resign and form a Premier League from the 1992/93 season. Promotion to the top flight next season would be crucial as the game was about to change forever.

Millwall would soon have to work out how they would do that - without Teddy Sheringham.

Barclays League Division Two 1990-91 Final Table

Oldham Athletic	**46**	**25**	**13**	**8**	**83**	**53**	**+30**	**88**	**Champions**
West Ham	**46**	**24**	**15**	**7**	**60**	**34**	**+26**	**87**	**Promoted**
Sheffield Wed	**46**	**22**	**16**	**8**	**80**	**51**	**+29**	**82**	**Promoted**
Notts County	**46**	**23**	**11**	**12**	**76**	**55**	**+21**	**80**	**Play-off winners**
Millwall	**46**	**20**	**13**	**13**	**70**	**51**	**+19**	**73**	
Brighton	46	21	7	18	63	69	−6	70	
Middlesbrough	46	20	9	17	66	47	+19	69	
Barnsley	46	19	12	15	63	48	+15	69	
Bristol City	46	20	7	19	68	71	−3	67	
Oxford United	46	14	19	13	69	66	+3	61	
Newcastle United	46	14	17	15	49	56	−7	59	
Wolves	46	13	19	14	63	63	0	58	
Bristol Rovers	46	15	13	18	56	59	−3	58	
Ipswich Town	46	13	18	15	60	68	−8	57	
Port Vale	46	15	12	19	56	64	−8	57	
Charlton Athletic	46	13	17	16	57	61	−4	56	
Portsmouth	46	14	11	21	58	70	−12	53	
Plymouth Argyle	46	12	17	17	54	68	−14	53	
Blackburn Rovers	46	14	10	22	51	66	−15	52	
Watford	46	12	15	19	45	59	−14	51	
Swindon Town	46	12	14	20	65	73	−8	50	
Leicester City	46	14	8	24	60	83	−23	50	
WBA	**46**	**10**	**18**	**18**	**52**	**61**	**−9**	**48**	**Relegated**
Hull City	**46**	**10**	**15**	**21**	**57**	**85**	**−28**	**45**	**Relegated**

91/92

millwall mick

5

Life Without Teddy

Teddy Sheringham's departure from Millwall was probably the single most predictable occurrence in the club's long history.

It's probably also fairly accurate to assume that not one single Millwall supporter begrudged the striker his deserved place in football's elite. There was obviously plenty of disappointment that he wasn't able to extend his record-equalling 38 goal season haul into the two disastrous play-off matches with Brighton so that he could fulfil that dream in a Millwall shirt.

Speculation had been rife since Nottingham Forest's FA Cup final defeat to Spurs that Clough would sign Sheringham and in July he did. There was no fuss, no scramble for his signature by a clutch of clubs waving their chequebooks so that Millwall could perhaps bank and extra few quid from the auction. It added some credibility to the argument that the deal had been done some time ago - and perhaps even before the play-offs, but there was neither proof of that or that it had any effect on Sheringham's contribution in the two matches. A claim that some fans had unfairly made in the bitter fallout of the failure to reach Wembley. For the vast majority of Millwall supporters, Sheringham had always given his all and shown the club loyalty beyond even their high expectations and he left with their blessing.

The reported fee was £2 million. Not a bad bit of business for the club, but two burning questions would be: How much of it would the club spend and on who?

Those questions were quickly answered when Rioch, who was proving he was no slouch in the transfer market, splashed out £100,000 on Crystal Palace's Phil Barber, £300,000 on Middlesbrough defender Colin Cooper and £400,000 on Hearts striker John Colquhoun. Rioch had been pursuing the Scottish international frontman - who had bagged 54 goals in 231 appearances for the Edinburgh club - for some six months and showed typical tenacity to get his man. He did some similarly smart business with Wrexham following a pre-season friendly. A young striker gave Millwall's back four a torrid time and Rioch was quick to offer £75,000 for the lightning-paced Chris Armstrong which the hard-up Division Four strugglers were happy to accept.

He then added to his midfield options by signing Ian Bogie from Preston. The former Newcastle man came through the Geordie side's youth ranks alongside a certain Paul Gascoigne and, with Paul Stephenson, they were considered three of the hottest young prospects in the game, Bogie apparently showing the most promise of the three. Two of them were now in Bruce Rioch's squad.

Fans' reactions to the flurry of transfer activity was mostly positive, although there were a few reservations about the signing of Barber from their rivals as such exchanges rarely worked out in Millwall's favour. He was however a very useful addition to the squad with two seasons of First Division football under his belt at Palace but had recently become a victim of the boo boys.

If anyone was still a bit miffed at transfer dealings between Millwall and Palace when the 91/92 season started, they'd be absolutely apoplectic twelves months later. The last signing, which used up almost exactly half of the Sheringham kitty certainly polarised opinion on The Den terraces.

Veteran striker Mark Falco was signed for £175,000 from QPR three days before the start of the season. It was a move which many felt was a waste of money and wages for a player clearly past his best and typical of what Millwall had always got wrong. Others felt it could be a shrewd bit of business bringing in a player who had always scored goals at the top level wherever he played - both north and south of the border. Time would tell.

Six of Rioch's new outfield recruits made their Millwall bows in the season opener away to Middlesbrough. They were joined by a new goalkeeper in Aidan Davison who had joined on a short-term deal after being released by Bury to provide cover with both first team choices Brian Horne and Keith Branagan injured.

The fans that made the long trip to Teesside watched their new look side lose by a single goal. Cooper, Colquhoun, Falco and Barber started the game with Armstrong and Bogie making substitute appearances.

By Rioch's admission the side lack cohesion and supporters could only hope that the age-old 'taking time to gel' justification that is used in such circumstances would quickly ring true.

That certainly seemed to be the case in the first home game of the season when any critics of the

Barber and Falco signings were quickly silenced.

First Barber lashed home from an Ian Dawes cross to give Millwall the lead over Sunderland in the fifteenth minute and five minutes later it was Falco's turn as he finished sweetly from a quick throughball that split the Sunderland defence.

Paul Kerr had quickly become a crowd favourite since his signing late on in the previous season. The fans loved his bustling all-action style that was bolstered with goals and he made it 3-1 on the half hour mark just sixty seconds after the visitors had thought they were back in it with a penalty. Barber scored again with another fierce drive on 70 minutes to make it 4-1 and put the seal on an impressive performance where Colquhoun in particular really shone.

The mood was bouyant, Rioch had plundered what looked to be a magical mix of experience and promise, speed and skill in his transfer dealings. What they needed this season over the last however was consistency and only time would tell if that was the case. Three games later and it looked like that Sunderland victory was nothing more than a freak and the only consistency in Millwall's game was defeat. Firstly the same team that had taken the Wearsiders apart so ruthlessly surrendered two first half goals away to a very ordinary Plymouth team.

Alex Rae pulled one back on the stroke of half time and they appeared to salvage something from the game when a Burrows own goal five minutes from time levelled the scores at 2-2 only for Millwall defender Steve Wood to put past his own 'keeper in injury time and hand the points to Plymouth.

Brighton were the next visitors to The Den but instead of revenge for that play-off double defeat, it was déjà vu as Robert Codnor again scored for the Seagulls in a 2-1 victory. Falco's second goal in as many home games was scant consolation for Rioch's men who were now just outside the relegation places - albeit with just four games played.

Not only did it open the old wound of that play-off disaster, it was the game where the club confirmed that Les Briley's contract had been cancelled. Briley had been the history-making captain that had led the team into the First Division for the first time in its history, but there was so much more to his Millwall career than that.

He made an instant impact when George Graham brought him to the club in 1984 and was an integral part of the 1985 promotion-winning side too. He made a solid start to Rioch's first full season but, like Kevin O'Callaghan (who Rioch chose not to offer a new deal to at the end of it) seemed to fall out of favour towards the season's end.

Briley had enjoyed a good working relationship with the two permanent Millwall managers he had played under before Rioch arrived - especially John Docherty and despite having also played under the famously strict Graham, he found Rioch's hard line approach a little to much.

"He had his disciplinarian way." Briley recalls, but there was more to it than just discipline:

"One day he said to me: 'I'm going to change this club'. My reply was: 'I don't think you will'."

Rioch clearly saw Briley as a threat to his authority. During the Docherty era, Briley - like many team captains - had acted almost as shop steward for his teammates, taking their concerns to The Doc.

The flipside of that of course was that Docherty often used this as leverage to find out what was going on among the ranks from Briley.

It was a potentially awkward set up but worked well. Certainly all the while things were going well at the club. Briley - now juggling the roles of team captain, club captain and PFA rep - realised early on that he wasn't going to be able to have that same relationship with Rioch: "We had a row at the training ground during his first season.

A few of the lads had come to me and said they weren't happy".

It wasn't hard to understand now why results on the pitch had taken a sudden downturn, Briley had fallen out of favour and there was such a high turnround of players.

Then, in his PFA duties helping players whose careers had been cut short through injury, they locked horns again:

"At the start of the following season Sean Sparham and Nicky Coleman had to retire through injury and there was a contract issue so once again I got dragged into the office. He asked me to sort it out, saying this is what I want to pay them but they won't accept it."

"I replied that I didn't blame them, and told him that it wasn't fair what he was offering so I'd need to get the PFA in. That was me gone. I got the PFA in, he didn't like that and I got a call a couple of weeks later informing me my contract was to be paid up."

Thankfully, such a loyal and successful servant to the club wasn't ushered out quite so shabbily by all:

"Reg Burr sent me a fabulous letter saying 'thank you for everything you've done'."

Even at 34, Briley wasn't short of suitors and quickly found himself a new club at the same level, ironically Brighton.

It was understandable that Rioch wanted to assemble his own team and not let sentimentality get in the way, but it appeared he was going about it in an increasingly robust way.

Newly-promoted Cambridge were the next visitors to SE16. John Beck's controversial direct tactics had won him few footballing friends but neither he nor the Cambridge fans cared because they had also won their side successive promotions in the last two seasons.

The last time Beck brought his side to The Den was in an FA Cup match two seasons before when the sides were at opposite ends of the league and, after a draw, the then Fourth Division Cambridge won the replay to knock First Division Millwall out. Now they were passing The Lions on the way up the Second Division table as once again Rioch's men showed their soft touch up against Beck's no-nonsense approach.

A fourth minute Paul Kerr penalty was quickly wiped out by Cheetham and, in the 74th minute, a 17-year-old defender making his league debut scored the winner. That young full-back was a certain Gary Rowett.

The match programme for that Cambridge match had some revelations about the Teddy Sheringham transfer. Bruce Rioch revealed that

Nottingham Forest's FA Cup final opponents Spurs had been keen to sign Sheringham but manager Terry Venables was only able to offer players plus cash as the cash-strapped club's coffers were almost bare. Rioch explained that the deal wasn't right because it provided neither the right players or amount of money for him and when Forest offered the full £2 million the deal was done.

Sheringham meanwhile had just netted his second goal for his new club and was already adjusting well to life back in the First Division.

Two more departures from The Den signalled the continuing shift from the old Docherty regime to the new one under Rioch. Midfielder Gary Waddock was released after failing to agree terms on a new deal and young midfielder Darren Morgan joined The Doc's Millwall reunion at Bradford alongside former Lions Treacy, Torpey Babb and Dowson.

Like his four new Bantam teammates, Morgan's departure was seen as a possible error on Rioch's part, turning his back on young, home-grown talent in favour of spending money on new recruits where there was a risk that they may not settle in to such a unique club and fanbase. Rioch clearly wanted his own team, but his shipping out of the old regime did nothing to quieten rumours that his uncompromising style was starting to turn the team against him.

The frustrating flimsiness of Millwall's performances was on show yet again away to bottom-of-the-table Oxford when, after taking complete control of the game through first half goals from Colquhoun and Rae, they allowed them back into it when ex-Lion Trevor Aylott returned to haunt them by pulling a goal back just before the break. Millwall were unable to regain control of the match in the second half and Melville's last-minute equaliser was as predictable as it was gut-wrenching.

Albert Einstein is credited with the saying: "The definition of insanity is doing the same thing over and over again and expecting a different result" and Rioch's side appeared to be attempting to demonstrate the great man's philosophy in their football.

Almost unbelievably, three days after turning three points into one in the 2-2 draw at Oxford, they did almost exactly the same at Bristol City. Two goals in a minute from Falco and Colquhoun put them in control just after half an hour but they managed to switch off enough to concede right on half time and hand the incentive over to City whose efforts to salvage a point were rewarded almost inevitably with a late leveller.

Rioch put both disappointing trips down to a mixture of bad luck and lack of concentration, which didn't fill Lions supporters with much encouragement for the battles ahead.

Unrest was once again spreading across the UK with unemployment hitting a three year high at 2.4 million. Riots erupted in Tyneside and the midlands and with Millwall now in the bottom three, the natives of south east London were growing a little restless too as they hosted an unlikely Second Division early season relegation six-pointer when fourth-bottom Newcastle visited The Den.

Barclays League Division Two - September 21st 1991

	P	W	D	L	F	A	PTS
21. Newcastle Utd	8	1	3	4	11	16	6
22. MILLWALL	**7**	**1**	**2**	**4**	**12**	**13**	**5**
23. Bristol Rovers	7	0	2	5	8	14	2
24. Oxford United	6	0	1	5	6	13	1

Grumbles of 'here we go again' began to filter through the sparsely-populated terraces when Ossie Ardiles' men took an eighth-minute lead through Neillson but fortunately, under Ardiles, Newcastle were playing a similar kamikaze brand of football to Millwall's and allowed Kerr to level soon after. The Lions' luck finally appeared to have changed for the better when Kerr struck again in the final minute to earn his side just their second win of the season.

It was a match that saw Millwall's two ex-Newcastle starlets start in the same team for the third time in a row. Ian Bogie - whose fee had been set by a transfer tribunal at £145,000, disappointing Preston who were after £250,000 - and Paul Stephenson who was returning from injury.

Bogie looked good on the ball, skillful, pacey and a great addition to the craft of Kerr, Colquhoun an Rae, all of whom were becoming fan favourites and at times during the Newcastle win, as in the only other victory so far against Sunderland, Millwall showed the quality of promotion contenders rather than bottom three battlers.

Yet there was still a brittle look to them defensively which was equally mystifying given the experience they had there with Dawes, Cooper, Wood and McCarthy. Something just wasn't quite right somehow.

After The Lord Mayor's Show

6

Keep Picking That Bogie

Millwall's third 2-2 draw in four games provided a refreshing twist to the recent pattern. Swindon visited The Den in a League Cup second round first leg and stormed into a 2-0 first half lead only to be pegged back by goals either side of the break from Rae and Armstrong.

It was Armstrong's first goal for the club and, being only 20, was being introduced gradually to the first team with some substitute appearances. Many fans felt his progress should be fast-tracked with injuries to the more experienced strikers John McGinlay and Phil Barber and he looked impressive with each introduction. His first goal for the club coincided with just his second start and only served to add weight to the argument to play him more. He was back on the bench for the trip to Barnsley where Rioch's caution may have been proved correct as Millwall continued their mini-revival with a 2-0 win. Alex Rae scored both goals and was looking more impressive with every match. The lively Scottish midfielder was also Millwall's poster boy for the announcement in the programme before the next match against Blackburn. The club had finally landed a shirt sponsorship deal after playing in either blank shirts or ones emblazoned somewhat apologetically with the club's name on them on and off for the past two seasons.

No formal explanation was ever given as to why the club stopped its original four year deal with Lewisham Council signed in 1987 after just two seasons and then decided to put them back on midway through the 90/91 campaign.

Neither were any reasons given for the bizarre appearance of 'MILLWALL' appearing on the front during the second half of the First Division relegation season, resembling a hastily printed budget souvenir for a stag weekend.

Now the players would wear the 'Fairview New Homes PLC' brand on their shirts in what was actually the next major stage in Millwall's plans to move away from The Den - even though this wasn't mentioned in the announcement.

Millwall's new Commercial Director Mike Ryan heralded the six figure, two-year deal as one of the biggest in the Second Division and part of a planned long-term working relationship with Fairview to improve the local environment.

What wasn't mentioned was that Fairview would be the ones building the new homes on the land currently occupied by The Den when Millwall moved to their new stadium in 1993. This deal, along with the land sale itself and the balance of the Teddy Sheringham money left over after Rioch's summer shopping spree would be used to cover the costs of building the 25,000 all-seater arena fit for the soon-to-be-launched Premier League.

What certainly wasn't fit for the new money-laden top flight was Millwall. They were easily beaten 3-1 by a Blackburn side who had shown similarly inconsistent form under caretaker manager Tony Parkes as Millwall but were much better organised in every department.

Three days later Millwall's involvement in the League Cup was ended with another 3-1 reverse in the second leg at Swindon despite taking the lead in the tie through an early Colquhoun strike. Their topsy turvy form continued at Southend where Millwall rarely enjoyed much luck over the years as they showed a little more resilience.

After falling behind to a 21st minute Sussex goal, Rae and Stephenson sent them into the break 2-1 up only for Tilson to level shortly after the restart. Finally though it was The Lions' turn to enjoy some last-minute luck and Colquhoun snatched a late winner.

It was a morale-boosting win watched by a rather unexpected spectator. With top flight games taking the weekend off due to England's European Championships qualifier with Turkey, Teddy Sheringham took the opportunity to watch his old teammates. Typically his appearance there was greeted by some good old fashioned Millwall humour when fans gave him a few choruses of "What a waste of money" and "Teddy get the beers in" after spotting him in the Roots Hall stands.

A creditable 0-0 draw at third-placed Ipswich showed encouraging signs of stability but then the exact same starting eleven travelled to Plymouth three days later only to be thrashed 4-0. It may have only been the ZDS Cup but was a worrying reminder of Millwall's split-personality.

Canadian rocker Bryan Adams was making history with his theme to Kevin Costner hit film 'Robin Hood'. *(Everything I do) I do it for you* was on its way to a record-breaking sixteen weeks at the top of the UK charts, but its perpetual playing on the radios of Millwall supporters wasn't the only annoying constant in their lives.

Another last-minute defeat followed when Ian Ormondroyd scored the late decider in a 2-1 home defeat to Derby and Millwall once again appeared to be more comfortable away from home than at The Den as a 2-0 win at Watford took them up to the dizzy heights of thirteenth.

The Den cash registers were ringing again when central defender Steve Wood was signed by First Division Southampton for £400,000 in what was no doubt another New Den down payment. The move meant that five of Millwall's Second Division title-winning team were now plying their trade in the top flight: Cascarino, Sheringham, Carter and Wood with Hurlock at Rangers north of the border. Cascarino had since moved from Aston Villa to join Celtic.

Chris Armstrong had started the Derby and Watford games and celebrated his third full appearance with a goal in the 1-1 home draw with Portsmouth and despite the setback of a 2-1 defeat away to Tranmere, Millwall finally seemed to be putting a little run together making it three wins in five with victories over Port Vale away and Wolves at home. What made The Lions' first back-to-back wins of the season all the more satisfying for Rioch was that they came courtesy of goals from summer signings Falco - who hit both in the 2-0 win at Vale Park - and Phil Barber

- who got the first in the 2-1 Wolves victory - as well as John McGinlay who was finally back from injury. McGinlay was on target again with a last minute goal to earn a 1-1 draw at Grimsby and extend the run to one defeat in six and edge into the top half of the table for the first time, but it was back to bad habits again when third-bottom Bristol Rovers visited The Den and left with all three points after a 1-0 win.

Away form was still their saviour though with that reverse at Tranmere just their third league defeat on the road all season and first since August.

Meanwhile, two of British popular culture's biggest names - for very different reasons - departed in November 1991. First Robert Maxwell was found dead after apparently falling from his yacht. Maxwell was the larger-than-life publishing magnate, head of the Mirror Group of newspapers and former nemesis of Reading and Oxford fans when he, as chairman of the latter, attempted to merge the two as 'Thames Valley Royals'.

Then Freddie Mercury, the flamboyant lead singer of Queen died after losing his much-speculated battle with HIV.

Millwall's encouraging away form continued in December with a 1-1 draw at promotion hopefuls

Leicester and they finally exacted revenge for that play-off loss over Brighton when they went to The Goldstone Ground next. This time it was Millwall's turn to score four and two more goals from McGinlay along with a Paul Kerr penalty and debut strike by Etienne Verveer sealed a thrilling 4-3 victory on the south coast against a Brighton side battling against relegation. Suriname-born Verveer - who quickly earned the fans' nickname 'ET' - had started his career at Dutch giants Ajax before playing in Switzerland with FC Chur where Millwall snapped him up from.

One possible reason for Millwall's success on the road might have been Ian Bogie. With teams committing more at home, Bogie was able to unlock defences on the break with a bit more success than at The Den where visiting teams often parked the bus. Bogie was certainly endearing himself to fans, who hadn't yet become tired of shouting at manager Bruce Rioch to "Keep picking that Bogie..."

Unfortunately Millwall's injury crisis which had deprived them of striker Falco just as he seemed to be finding form, had now claimed Bogie and the stark contrast between Millwall's solid away displays and shocking home performances was never clearer than when Watford visited The Den on Boxing Day.

Just five days after that brilliant display of attacking football at Brighton, Rioch's limp Lions were trounced 4-0 by a Watford side lying fourth bottom in the Second Division table.

Third-bottom Plymouth then visited two days later and the home fans finally lost their patience with their side as boos filled the air when Morgan put the struggling Devon club ahead after 25 minutes. For the first time in his short reign, Bruce Rioch was starting to be doubted.

Fortunately for Rioch goals from McCarthy and McGinlay either side of half time gave his side only their fourth home win of the campaign but nevertheless some respite to at least end 1991 on a relative high spot and mid-table respectability.

Speculation was surrounding an approach for Alex Rae from both Nottingham Forest and Everton but Rioch was quick to dismiss the rumours. Fans were however starting to become uneasy that the club was in danger of reverting back to its old ways of selling off its best players at the first approach.

1992 would see work start on Millwall's new stadium at Senegal Fields so the pressure was well and truly on to finance the project. It also began to increase on Bruce Rioch, starting with a flurry of goals - in all directions.

7

Pompey Crimes

There was more than just a new year hangover feel about Millwall's trip to Swindon on the opening day of 1992. The travelling fans that braved the chilly trip to the west country will have been feeling a fresh nausea by half time as their team crumbled to trail 3-0.

John McGinlay's fifth goal in eight games was the only score in the second half as The Lions handed Swindon an easy three points, but Millwall's roller coaster season would take another high turn three days later when they were on the road again, this time to Third Division promotion-hopefuls Huddersfield in the FA Cup.

By the time the referee's whistle signalled the end of the first half at Leeds Road it was Millwall who had gone nap with an impressive 4-0 lead which included a goal from Dave Thompson, two from Alex Rae and a landmark strike from new boy Verveer, The impressive Dutch ball-master became the first Millwall player for 30 years to score on both his league and FA Cup debut. The last had been Pat Terry whose goals were split over the 61-62 and 62-63 seasons. Before that, the last Lions player to do it in the same season was Angus Morrison in 1957.

Huddersfield had rarely been a happy hunting ground for The Lions and the tie posed a potential shock given Millwall's leaky defence which had shipped eleven goals in their last three matches and the home side's lofty league position - albeit in the division below. Once again however, Rioch's team had pulled a surprise win on the road out of the bag. A week later they hit the buffers again though - and in spectacular fashion once more.

In their third away match on the spin, they travelled to Roker Park to face a Sunderland side who were three places below Millwall in fifteenth and that they had beaten 4-1 at The Den in the season's home opener.

The match was finely poised at 1-1 going into half time, with Alex Rae cancelling out Hardyman's opener but Rioch's ragged 'Wall were blitzed by three goals in three minutes just after half time - one from John Byrne and two from Don Goodman. Goodman was able to complete his hat-trick with twenty minutes to spare before the shellshocked Lions grabbed a consolation goal with ten left. There was still time however for Davenport to end a thoroughly humiliating afternoon for Millwall, scoring Sunderland's sixth in the final minutes.

That crushing 6-2 reverse took Millwall's goals conceded to seventeen in their last five league matches and was the worst possible preparation for their first home match of the New Year against third-placed Middlesbrough.

Once again though Millwall upset the odds and put in a thoroughly efficient display against Boro, who were now managed by former Charlton boss Lenny Lawrence for whom defeat at the hands of Millwall will have been nothing new. A goal in each half by McGinlay and Rae with thankfully none conceded gave Millwall fans hope that some consistency and discipline at the back could finally be built on with another promotion-challenger in Ipswich to visit The Den next.

Those same old bad habits reappeared though and John Lyall's Ipswich cantered to a 3-0 lead by the hour mark before Millwall could so much as muster a serious threat to The Tractor Boys' goal. Late goals from Rae and Kerr only served to give the result the inaccurate appearance that Millwall had ever been in with a chance to gain anything from yet another defeat, and three more goals conceded.

FA Cup interest was ended at the hands of First Division Norwich away next. Mercifully it was by the more modest scoreline of 2-1 which probably came as some relief to Millwall's weary fans who may have been fearing another heavy loss to the top flight Canaries.

Millwall's Scots double act of McGinlay and Rae were the only constant it seemed in what was becoming a frustrating season of taking one step forwards and then two back. With Malcolm Allen and Mark Falco both long-term injury casualties and fellow Scot John Colquhoun also on the treatment table, McGinlay and Rae's goals were helping to keep Millwall away from the danger zone.

As with Middlesbrough at home, the deadly duo were on target again in another 2-0 victory, this time away to Derby where striker Jon Goodman made his comeback from a lay-off. It was Millwall's sixth away victory of the season - not bad for mid-February considering the crippling injury list and sieve-like defence. It was just a shame they had only managed five wins at The Den. Something which would surely be put right with the visit of struggling Grimsby.

The Den was stunned when Rees gave the lowly

Mariners a first minute lead and whilst Rae was on target again to level it up on the half hour, there was nothing more for Lions fans than frustration at Millwall's inability to go on and win the game as Grimsby shut up shop and left with a valuable point.

It seemed that lessons still hadn't been learned when at Bristol Rovers - who were becoming something of a jinx team for Millwall - The Lions found themselves a goal down before their fans had chance to blow on their Bovril. Goodman made it 1-1 at the break only for Mehew to restore The Pirates' lead soon after. In a final ten minutes that was so typical of Millwall's season, Chris Armstrong made an immediate impact, making it 2-2 just five minutes after being introduced. Just when it seemed Millwall would take a hard-earned point back to south east London, the unlucky Phil Barber scored a last-minute own goal to hand the points to Bristol Rovers and leave Millwall with just two league wins in seven games.

Charlton visited The Den next in what would be the first of two quickfire meetings between the local rivals with Millwall travelling to Upton Park ten days later where The Addicks were currently ground sharing with West Ham.

Steve Gritt had got Charlton in good shape

following the departure of Lennie Lawrence and they arrived at The Den in eighth place, confident of a rare win against The Lions. Millwall fans could only pray that the right version of their team turned up to spare them more humiliation.

Thankfully it did and a first half penalty by Paul Kerr was enough to give Rioch's men a 1-0 win. They followed that up with another impressive home win over fifth placed Leicester with first half goals from Colin Cooper and Jon Goodman earning them a 2-0 win and incredibly, their first back-to-back clean sheets of the season - a stat which had taken them 33 matches.

That win made it three in the last five and the defence was starting to look a little stronger with that aberration at Bristol Rovers the only glitch. Their run of form may have come at just the right time with players returning from injury and now just six points separating Millwall in 12th place from that final play-off spot.

It was just three between them and tenth-placed Charlton who were on a three-match losing streak when Millwall faced them at Upton Park and with mid-table Tranmere next at The Den and a trip to ninth-placed Portsmouth, The Lions destiny was very much in their hands if they wanted to give themselves something to play for in the final ten game run-in.

What instead transpired over the course of those three football matches led to the end of Bruce Rioch's short reign at The Den.

Trips to Upton Park were rare and often fruitless for Millwall fans, but this was Charlton they were facing and, after finally finding some form of consistency for the first time in an eventful season, confidence was high that their team could make it three wins out of three. At the same time they could consign Charlton's play-off hopes to the bin with a fourth defeat in a row and start to mount a genuine promotion challenge. Something that had seemed miles away following that 6-2 drubbing at Sunderland.

When Hendry struck the only goal of the match for Charlton with five minutes left, Millwall's season was once again thrown into reverse. Four days later they surrendered tamely to a very ordinary Tranmere side at The Den. In a match where everything that could go wrong did, the Wirral side punished Rioch's hapless Lions almost at will with first half goals from Morrissey and veteran striker John Aldridge. Aldridge added a third without reply and the fans' patience finally snapped. Rioch's days were numbered, but not before another drubbing - this time on the south coast.

Millwall's Fratton Park nightmare began in the

third minute when Martin Kuhl gave Pompey the lead which was doubled three minutes later by Guy Whittingham. It was three by half time when Whittingham added his second but this time there would be no stoic rearguard action to counter a first half collapse from Millwall.

Within ten minutes of the restart Whittingham had his treble to make it 5-0, three minutes after McLoughlin had started the second half rout. There were genuine fears of Millwall's record defeat being equalled when Burns made it six with twenty minutes still remaining but mercifully Portsmouth took their foot off the gas and Etienne Verveer was able to strike a late consolation.

It had been one of Millwall's most torrid ninety minutes of football in many seasons. They had been beaten heavily before during this difficult season but the defeats to Sunderland and Watford paled into insignificance compared to the sorry show on the south coast.

Admittedly there was little Millwall's defence could do about Kuhl's opener - a screamer from 30 yards - but he was allowed an age and acres of space to get his shot away. Whittingham was able to walk through the Millwall back line for the second and the third was a comedy of errors which saw Keith Stevens and 'keeper Aidan

Davison contrive to get in each other's way dealing with a routine ball and Whittingham couldn't believe his luck as they presented him with the ball at his feet and an open goal.

McLoughlin's fourth came after an almighty scramble in the Millwall goalmouth where The Lions were simply second to every battle for the ball and Whittingham completed probably the easiest hat-trick of his career when Stevens again failed to complete a simple pass back to Davison and left him with another tap-in.

What was all the more galling about the two errors between Stevens and Davison was the new rule that prevented goal keepers from picking up back passes was still a few months away!

It was tough on Stevens who was now one of the few surviving heroes from those heady First Division days and returning from another injury layoff and looked some way off the pace.

Burns was waiting with teammate Steve Wigley on the Millwall penalty spot as The Lions' back four again went AWOL and they almost had time to toss a coin to decide who was going to put the finish touch on an unchallenged cross to make it 6-0.

Ironically by far the best goal of the game was Millwall's. Malcolm Allen made a welcome return and held the ball up nicely before laying if off for

Stevens who was making one of his trademark runs down the right. His pinpoint cross was met spectacularly with a glorious diving header from Verveer. It was of course far too little, too late.

Probably the most frustrating thing for Millwall fans was that they had been well and truly taken apart by a Pompey side playing almost identical football to that which had thrilled them four seasons before and won promotion to the First Division. It was high tempo, often direct, but also pleasing to the eye at times with neat, nippy wing play. It was also of course very effective. Millwall had spent the last three seasons trying to move away from that mode of play having felt as though they had been 'found out' after one season of success in the top flight. Now, back in Division Two, it was clear that it had a place again. You only had to look at John Beck's Cambridge who had it off to a tee and were riding high in the top three to see proof of that.

Millwall meanwhile had developed something of an identity crisis with their style of play. It was completely indiscernible most of the time, with many players looking lost, unaware of their role or how to react in basic footballing situations. On other albeit rare occasions, they were a delight to watch and quite devastating on the attack.

As with all such capitulations, questions were

being asked right up from the beleaguered fans on the coaches, trains and cars travelling back along the M27 to the directors and chairman in the Millwall boardroom.

In one of his last programme notes, Rioch explained how in a recent interview he was asked what he liked and disliked about being a football manager. In typical straight-talking fashion, he concluded that he liked winning and disliked losing. They are of course the only factors that decide your fate as a football manager and this season Rioch had lost too many.

He had also lost his last game in charge of Millwall. Three days after the drubbing at Portsmouth his resignation was tendered and accepted by the Millwall board. As the country prepared to go to the polls and vote in the next general election, Millwall were on the lookout for a new manager.

After The Lord Mayor's Show

8

Mick Caretaker

◇◇◇◇◇◇◇◇◇◇◇◇◇◇◇◇◇◇◇◇◇◇◇◇◇◇◇◇◇

Within 24 hours of Bruce Rioch's resignation being announced, Millwall moved quickly to appoint a caretaker manager for the remaining ten matches of the season. There was little surprise that the new man in the Millwall dugout was Mick McCarthy.

He revealed in his first programme notes for the home match with Port Vale that he'd been shocked to get the call from the Millwall Chairman. Reg Burr invited him along to his West End office for a chat and promptly gave him the opportunity to start his football management career - something he admitted he was looking to do at a time when it was looking increasingly likely that a recent knee injury would spell the end of his playing days.

Millwall had tried a manager with a track record

at the level they were playing at and it had failed. Although they had come very close, the very nature of how they missed out on promotion via the play-offs in Rioch's first season really encapsulated his bitter sweet stay at the club.

Now they were trying the hungry young first-timer. McCarthy had played at the highest level in three countries and captained at a World Cup finals so experience as a player - and the knowledge he would have undoubtedly picked up from playing under the likes of Jack Charlton, Billy McNeil and Raymond Domenech - could prove invaluable. Millwall fans would need some convincing though and the Lions' board of directors' hearts must have sank when the 1-0 win over Port Vale to mark McCarthy's first match in charge was watched by the third lowest attendance of the season - just over 6,000.

The winning goal was scored by Malcolm Allen whose return to full fitness must have been a big boost to McCarthy - as well as the clean sheet. Always important for a defender. That much-needed defensive discipline was still in evidence in his first away game too - a creditable 0-0 draw at Wolves.

Even in the face of his first set-back he came good. Struggling Oxford took an early lead which they held on to until ten minutes after the break but Millwall remained composed and goals from Stephenson and Goodman turned the match around to give McCarthy seven points from his first three matches.

In stark contrast to Rioch, he showed he had a lighter side by asking the players to go back out onto The Den pitch for a warm-down afterwards. After they had all filed somewhat puzzled back on to the hallowed turf and awaited instruction, McCarthy remained in the dressing room and only when the floodlights had been switched off leaving them in darkness and returning to the dressing room to find out what was going on did a smirking McCarthy remind them of the date: Wednesday, April 1st!

The match was watched by Millwall's lowest crowd of the season of 5,946 - their lowest league gate since November 1987 - and it would get worse with neither a place in the play-offs or a relegation escape to fight for. Even in these new play-off days when few teams' seasons were over until the last match or so, Millwall were coasting and wasn't big box office.

It was of course handy for McCarthy, allowing him to fully explore every possible player formation and work out, should he get the job on a permanent basis, which way to go next season. Victory over Oxford was followed by McCarthy's first taste of defeat against Cambridge. There was certainly no shame in the narrow 1-0 away loss to John Beck's team who had hit the top of the table and were looking a good bet, incredibly, to be one of the inaugural members of next season's new FA Premier League and completing their climb from Division Four to the new top flight in success seasons.

A Dion Dublin goal was all that separated the sides and Millwall continued to look a completely different defensive prospect when they took an early lead through Malcolm Allen in the next home game against Swindon. It finished 1-1 and there was a first home blip as an Andy Cole-inspired Bristol City inflicted McCarthy's first Den defeat, but on the bright side the slightly healthier crowd of just under 7,000 was an encouraging marker that Lions fans were as impressed with the new regime as the players seemed to be.

The Conservatives won the general election with a reduced majority, forcing the Labour leader Neil Kinnock to resign, but it was number nine for Millwall that was catching the eye again rather than number ten on Downing Street.

Malcolm Allen grabbed his third goal in five as McCarthy's hungry Lions completed a double over Newcastle with another disciplined display at St James Park. The 1-0 win made it a third clean sheet in the new manager's seven games in charge. Allen was on target again in a 1-1 home draw with Barnsley but there was no avoiding a third defeat in their final away game of the season at play-off chasing Blackburn. The season did end on a bright note however with a 2-0 win at home to Southend and the fact that Millwall's last five goals of the campaign had been scored by either Malcolm Allen or Chris Armstrong was a major boost as McCarthy started to shape his preferred starting eleven for the next campaign.

For the first time that season, Millwall fans could see a settled line-up being established and it was paying dividends. It did seem a little harsh that their final position of 15th was their lowest since November but small details like that didn't phase McCarthy. He had passed his first major test as a football manager in safely negotiating his first ten games in charge as caretaker.

Elsewhere in the league, Cambridge's gallant attempt to make it from Fourth to First Division in successive seasons ran out of steam and they missed out in the play-offs, but it must have been galling for Millwall fans to see Middlesbrough manage to succeed in regaining top flight status where Millwall had failed. The final Football League top flight season saw Manchester United squander a golden opportunity to win their first title in 25 years and were pipped by rivals Leeds. Notts County and West Ham made an immediate return to the second tier which would be renamed Division One from the next season. At Nottingham Forest, who finished eighth, Teddy Sheringham was top scorer with 20 goals in all competitions.

So Millwall were back in Division One, but not in the way they had hoped. Now that the Premier League had begun, the real money would start to flow into the game and a gap start to open between the top flight and the rest of the league. It was more important than ever for The Lions to make it back to the top division. For proof of this, you had to look no further than Blackburn Rovers. They had been taken over by multi-millionaire fan Jack Walker the previous season and invested heavily in promotion to the top flight which they achieved via the play-offs. But that was just the start.

Making Mick McCarthy permanent manager was a no-brainer for the Millwall board. His next task was much bigger.

In Millwall's last ever season at Then Den before their move to a brand new purpose-built stadium ready for the new Premier League, could he deliver Premier League football to play in it?

Barclays League Division Two 1991-92 Final Table

Ipswich Town	**46**	**24**	**12**	**10**	**70**	**50**	**+20**	**84**	**Champions**
Middlesbrough	**46**	**23**	**11**	**12**	**58**	**41**	**+17**	**80**	**Promoted**
Derby County	46	23	9	14	69	51	+18	78	
Leicester City	46	23	8	15	62	55	+7	77	
Cambridge	46	19	17	10	65	47	+18	74	
Blackburn Rovers	**46**	**21**	**11**	**14**	**70**	**53**	**+17**	**74**	**Play-off winners**
Charlton Athletic	46	20	11	15	54	48	+6	71	
Swindon Town	46	18	15	13	69	55	+14	69	
Portsmouth	46	19	12	15	65	51	+14	69	
Watford	46	18	11	17	51	48	+3	65	
Wolves	46	18	10	18	61	54	+7	64	
Southend United	46	17	11	18	63	63	0	62	
Bristol Rovers	46	16	14	16	60	63	−3	62	
Tranmere Rovers	46	14	19	13	56	56	0	61	
Millwall	**46**	**17**	**10**	**19**	**64**	**71**	**−7**	**61**	
Barnsley	46	16	11	19	46	57	−11	59	
Bristol City	46	13	15	18	55	71	−16	54	
Sunderland	46	14	11	21	61	65	−4	53	
Grimsby Town	46	14	11	21	47	62	−15	53	
Newcastle United	46	13	13	20	66	84	−18	52	
Oxford United	46	13	11	22	66	73	−7	50	
Plymouth Argyle	**46**	**13**	**9**	**24**	**42**	**−22**		**48**	**Relegated**
Brighton	**46**	**12**	**11**	**23**	**56**	**77**	**−21**	**47**	**Relegated**
Port Vale	**46**	**10**	**15**	**21**	**42**	**59**	**−17**	**45**	**Relegated**

After The Lord Mayor's Show

92/93

farewell old friend...

9

The Final Countdown

◇◇◇◇◇◇◇◇◇◇◇◇◇◇◇◇◇◇◇◇◇◇◇◇◇◇◇◇◇◇

The 1992-93 season was one that most Millwall fans probably didn't want to happen. The usually excitable build-up to the season's opener was strangely subdued. This would be a season that no Lions fan had ever experienced before, completely regardless of the final league position. It would be a 26-match countdown to the end of their beloved Den, with every passing game marked as "the last time we'll see us play them down here...".

Some fans were in denial, some still irked at the club's inability to simply modernise The Den, a small minority were accepting of the situation and looking forward to the move signalling a new era for the club. It still didn't feel real - especially with so many previous false dawns, but a visit to the site of the new stadium where work was progressing at a rapid rate, would confirm this really was happening and everyone had to get on with it.

Elsewhere, evidence that Millwall needed to make sacrifices and move the club forward if they wanted to regain a place in the game's elite came in the shape of newly-promoted Blackburn Rovers.

Jack Walker was already starting to splash his cash and the team that had come from mid-table to win the play-offs and promotion to the newly-formed, money-laden Premier League shocked the football world by spending £3.6 million on Southampton striker Alan Shearer. It was the first sign of the buying power afforded to clubs with the new television deal that had been signed with Sky. They had blown previous big spenders ITV out of the water and taken live coverage of the top flight to a new level - and away from terrestrial television. Millwall needed to be in on this party before it was too late because it was clear that before long, a gap would open up.

If Millwall's supporters were going into the new season in a bit of a daze, it looked to be rubbing off on the players. Lions stopper Aidan Davison became the one of the first to suffer at the hands of the new rule that goalkeepers were not allowed to pick up back passes when he fumbled in the opener away to Watford to gift them a penalty equaliser. This came after his opposite number Perry Suckling had come a cropper to the new legislation to allow John McGinlay to give Millwall a twelfth minute lead. Things didn't improve for The Lions and they slumped to a 3-1 defeat.

What was troubling for fans was the summer sale of two players that were rare bright spots in the disappointing previous season. Paul Kerr and John Colquhoun departed for Port Vale and Sunderland respectively and in his first programme notes of the season, manager Mick McCarthy didn't attempt to sugar-coat it:

"The club's financial position meant we had to raise some cash and they were the only two we received acceptable offers for."

But they wouldn't be the last.

Also leaving was young defender Dave Thompson who joined Bristol City and striker Mark Falco who retired. Fairly unremarkable incomings were midfielder Andy May from Bristol City, defender Tony McCarthy (no relation) from Shelbourne and Paul Holsgrove from Dutch club FC Heracles.

In those notes, McCarthy pointed out that neither Kerr or Colquhoun had been available for selection during his caretaker spell in charge and that he had completely changed the team's playing style - of which May would prove to be an integral part - so if the story of Millwall selling off their good players to pay the bills was the same old one, at least the approach from the young manager was refreshingly new.

That opening day defeat at Watford was quickly wiped out when Oxford were beaten at The Den by the same score and Millwall fans had reason to be encouraged by their side's new shape with McGinlay up front with Armstrong providing a potent and pacey attack and a balance of youth, experience, craft and strength in a midfield of May, Barber, Malcolm Allen and Andy Roberts.

Roberts had quickly progressed through the youth ranks and had the look of a player with a footballing brain way in advance of his raw years.

The Oxford win also saw a American Kasey Keller in goal for The Lions. He had made his debut in the final day win over Southend the previous season and looked a solid last line of defence behind a back four of Dawes, Cunningham, Cooper and Stevens.

Four days after the Oxford victory, The Den saw another as Leyton Orient were brushed aside 3-0 in a League Cup first round second leg win where the lively Armstrong struck his second in successive matches.

What Millwall fans didn't need now after this

encouraging start was to lose any more of their key players. But that is exactly what happened, and in the worst possible fashion.

"After a reserve game, I spoke to someone in my office about players who might be available and Chris' name came up." McCarthy explained.

"I told him that I did not want to sell Chris, but he kept pressing me for a figure so to put an end to it I said I wouldn't be prepared to let him go for less than a million quid. I was stunned to go into my office a few days later find a bid of that order on my desk."

McCarthy went on to explain that neither he nor chairman Reg Burr wanted Armstrong to leave but felt they were in an impossible position. The deal was done and a lightning-quick striker in good form was allowed to leave the club striving for promotion before August was out - to local rivals Crystal Palace.

"We got a good deal" McCarthy reflected, remembering that Millwall had paid Wrexham just £75,000 for Armstrong a year earlier. That wouldn't have cut any ice with fans who could see this transaction for everything that it was: another part of the stadium-funding fire sale. This was borne out by the fact that considerable funds had now flowed into the club's coffers for Sheringham, Kerr, Colquhoun and Armstrong in the last twelve months with just a fraction of it spent.

Part of the deal that saw Armstrong make the leap from Division Four to Premier League in one and a bit seasons was young Palace striker Jamie Moralee making the reverse journey.

No-one had heard of him at Millwall, and it did little to calm the fury that yet again their local rivals were benefitting from their best players Many were still bitter over the transfer of Derek Possee to Palace twenty years before!

It was impossible to escape the Armstrong deal in the programme that day. Moralee boldly proclaimed that he'd score more goals than Armstrong in his first interview and chairman Burr, pictured in his familiar pose stood at the terrace crush barriers - surely for one of the last such photo opportunities at the old place - explained the finer points of the deal.

A £1,000,000 cash payment was the first part, with a further £500,000 if Armstrong went on to be capped for England. Palace also stumped up Wrexham's sell-on entitlement. Then of course there was the Moralee part of the deal.

It all added up to look like Palace felt they were still getting a bargain. Burr pointed out that they were offered other players but, acting on the advice of ex-Palace man and current assistant to

McCarthy Ian Evans, they insisted on Moralee. One of the other players offered was a certain Stan Collymore, but Millwall opted for Moralee and Southend stepped in to snap up the striker. Collymore's opportunity to make an impression on Millwall fans would come eventually though.

The bit that every fan would have read with a cynical nod of the head however was when Burr explained that the club was losing money every season because their expenses outstripped the revenue from the turnstiles. This was a clear message that not only was such business essential to make the move to the new stadium, but that fans had to swallow their angst and fill the new place to stop it happening again in the future.

On the pitch however, Millwall were proving that maybe they didn't need Armstrong after all.

Goals from McGinlay and Goodman gave them all three points against Swindon, followed by a solid goalless home draw against early promotion hopefuls Birmingham. The defence once again showed its discipline with another shut-out in another draw at Peterborough and the steady progress up the table and into those all-important play-off places was competed in fine style with a 6-0 thrashing of Notts County. Braces from Barber and Allen plus Goodman and a debut goal from promising youngster Tony Dolby had

The Den regulars asking: "Chris who?"

The cup draw had finally been kind too, with Arsenal being drawn in a two-legged second round League Cup affair. The opener at Highbury saw Millwall take the lead through Andy Roberts early in the second half. It was cancelled out by Kevin Campbell but The Lions left with a creditable draw and a mouth-watering second leg at The Den to come.

Sadly it was overshadowed by controversy as Arsenal striker Ian Wright appeared to be felled by a coin thrown form Millwall supporters. Television footage showed Wright go down but evidence of any actual missile wasn't as obvious. The striker insisted he had been struck but no coin was retrieved by the match officials and Wright did not appear to show any signs of being struck. It didn't matter to the press of course and all the headlines were about the incident rather than Millwall's performance.

Their top six place was cemented with a 1-1 draw at Brentford where Allen was again on target as he found a return to the form he'd enjoyed on his arrival at the club.

A 1-1 Anglo-Italian Cup draw away to Portsmouth did a little to exorcise the ghost of that 6-1 drubbing at the end of Rioch's reign and also gave McCarthy a chance to hand Holsgrove and his namesake debuts for the club.

It was also a first match for Moralee as McCarthy looked to ease his new young striker into the squad. September ended with Millwall nicely tucked in to sixth place in the table and Arsenal next to visit The Den.

McCarthy clearly felt Moralee's progress would be swift because by the time George Graham made his return to his old stomping ground with his Arsenal side, Millwall had sold the other half of their season-starting first choice front two.

John McGinlay had been allowed to join Secobnd Division (the new name for Division Three) Bolton where Bruce Rioch was now manager. The Scot had regularly been among the goals and it was another puzzling move in Lions fans' eyes, especially when the player admitted he had accepted the move because McCarthy couldn't guarantee him regular first team football.

He'd made a goalscoring start to the season but had been displaced by the fit-again Jon Goodman and McCarthy clearly felt more comfortable with Moralee challenging 'Elvis' for that place. The old Rioch guard was quickly being shipped out.

One of the few remaining players from John Docherty's First Division team was also soon to be on his way out with Brian Horne on loan at Middlesbrough where he made a handful of top flight appearances before being displaced by the fit-again Stephen Pears. He then made another loan move but this time down a division rather than up to Lou Macari's Second Division promotion-chasing Stoke. His Den days were clearly numbered with Kasey Keller now having a firm grip on the first team goalkeeping gloves.

Another of the survivors of those distant top flight days was Ian Dawes who was now a key member of McCarthy's well-drilled back four. After another 1-1 draw against Arsenal where a Lee Dixon own goal levelled Kevin Campbell's opener, the match ended 2-2 on aggregate after extra time and Dawes scored the only spot-kick for The Lions as they exited somewhat unfortunately 3-1 on penalties.

Back in league action Millwall had slipped from sixth to eleventh. A 2-0 defeat at Sunderland before the Arsenal cup match was followed by McCarthy's men finding themselves 2-0 down at home to Cambridge after just thirty minutes but goals from Allen and Goodman got them back into the game before the break and the game finished 2-2.

Neighbours Charlton had made a good start to the season and had occupied a top four spot until Millwall visited their temporary Upton Park home and, in front of the live TV cameras, Jamie

Moralee marked his first league start for the club with the second goal in a thoroughly professional 2-0 win. In a throw back to the old 'The Big Match' days, ITV were now regionalising their coverage and 'The London Match' showed highlights of a game each weekend - with commentary from the superb Brian Moore to complete the retro feel and add that inimitable Moore style.

It was a match that Millwall controlled from the start with Andy May pulling the strings at the back of McCarthy's midfield diamond midfield and Malcolm Allen tormenting Charlton from the front of it.

Alex Rae was back to his marauding best and gave The Lions the lead from 20 yards towards the end of a Millwall-dominant first half.

Moralee's debut strike was a typical poaching striker's goal, sliding in to be first on the end of Malcolm Allen's cross to the edge of the six yard box.

The game was also notable for the atmosphere it was played in. Charlton had provided free tickets for local school children who were forcing Moore's commentary to battle with an almost constant high-pitched chant of "Charlton, Charlton" throughout the match giving it more of a feel of a Bros concert than a London derby.

Millwall - and Moralee - repeated the feat a

week later when Wolves visited The Den but the Bristol Rovers jinx continued to prevent The Lions from breaking back into that coveted top six with a 1-0 defeat.

Rovers' neighbours City were Millwall's next opponents and this time McCarthy's men really went to town. In a breathtaking start, The Lions were four-nil ahead after half an hour thanks to goals from Cooper, Allen, May and Moralee's third in four. Andy Cole pulled one back on the stroke of half time but the match finished 4-1 and Millwall were almost back in the top six again. The match saw a debut for striker John Byrne, and it was seen as something of a coup for McCarthy to sign the Republic of Ireland international who had scored goals for both Sunderland and Brighton.

Andy May was quickly endearing himself to the Millwall faithful and his strike from 20 yards to make it 3-0 was no more than the midfield workaholic deserved.

The player who was really catching the eye though was Moralee. He was pacey, tough and most importantly, ruthless when presented with even a half chance of a goal.

It was a ruthlessness that would bring rewards again in the next match at Derby who had led since the 35th minute through Pembridge but when Moralee hit his fourth in five starts since making his debut on the hour, there was only ever going to be one winner and Alex Rae struck the winner two minutes later to set up a tasty Den promotion clash with West Ham.

Brian Moore and co were in attendance to cover the match live for The London Match and were proving something of a good luck charm for Millwall. It was a match that saw Keith Stevens sidle up closer to Lions legends Harry Cripps and Barry Kitchener with his 400th appearance for the club in all competitions.

Rhino, like Colin Cooper, had been converted from full back to a central defensive role by McCarthy and, along with his diamond midfield system, it was proving a huge success.

After a cagey opening 40 minutes the match started to grow increasingly bad tempered with tackles flying in - and Millwall coming out of most on top. Right-back Kenny Cunningham was enjoying lots of room to run into and make dangerous crosses into the West Ham box but on this occasion he decided to drive into the Hammer's penalty area where Robson, in-keeping with the spirit of the game - made a full-blooded challenge to upend the young Irishman and the referee had no hesitation in pointing to the spot.

Allen despatched the spot-kick ruthlessly high

and hard to Luděk Miklośko's top left corner and Millwall had the lead going into the break. The Lions went straight for their rivals from the start of the second half and just ten minutes in, a mazy Moralee run put Allen through. His shot was deflected by a West Ham defender but only as far as Phil Barber who gleefully slotted past Miklośko to put Millwall in control.

Even a late Robson goal couldn't prevent Millwall's third win in a row and send them up to fifth, right behind Billy Bonds' boys. Byrne got his first goal for the club to snatch a point from a 1-1 draw at Luton but there was disappointment at Portsmouth again when they came away with an unfortunate 1-0 defeat from Fratton Park.

Newcastle - who were Millwall's next away opponents, were running away with it at the top of the table, but it was very much game on for that second place and the value in those home wins against Wolves and West Ham was there for all to see:

Barclays League Division One - November 28th 1992							
	P	**W**	**D**	**L**	**F**	**A**	**PTS**
1. Newcastle Utd	18	15	1	2	28	14	46
2. Tranmere Rovers	18	10	4	4	32	20	34
3. West Ham	18	10	3	5	36	17	33
4. Swindon Town	19	9	6	4	36	28	33
5. Wolves	19	8	8	3	31	20	32
6. MILLWALL	**18**	**8**	**6**	**4**	**28**	**16**	**30**

The three victories in a row were matched with a trio of winless games when Barber was on target again in a 1-1 draw with Southend at The Den but Moralee's minor goal drought ended in style at home to Grimsby when he struck his first brace for the club in an impressive 2-1 win and he was on hand again to give his side a 1-0 half time advantage at runaway leaders Newcastle, only for Kevin Keegan's side to level the match with a very harsh penalty award.

Meanwhile there were more comings and goings as McCarthy continued to shape his squad. Going, and then coming back again was defender Alan McLeary. He'd spent a loan spell at First Division Wimbledon on the understanding that, if The Dons wanted to make the move permanent, the fee would be £300,000.

Crazy Gang boss Joe Kinnear did indeed want to relieve Millwall of yet another of their historic First Division team, but pleaded poverty saying the cash-strapped side could only afford £200,000. McCarthy's rebuff and assessment that the reduced offer was "taking the mick" would have encouraged Millwall fans that maybe the fire sale was off.

There was still interest in McLeary though and Peter Reid was keen to take him to Manchester City on a three month loan deal for the Premier

League side but once again a deal couldn't be agreed. One star of the top flight days who was off though was Paul Stephenson who joined Gillingham on loan, although McCarthy was quick to reassure fans that the move was more for the Geordie winger to get games under his belt after losing his place in the starting eleven.

Brian Horne was certainly getting around. His loan spell at Stoke ended and saw him make a similar move to Sunderland meaning he had now appeared in three divisions in three months.

A solid draw away to Tranmere who were proving the surprise package of the season and were tucked in behind Newcastle in the top two saw Millwall go into their final match of 1992 at home to Leicester in fourth place. An opening goal from Moralee made it four in five again for him and the increasingly impressive Goodman sealed a 2-0 win to take The Lions into 1993 in good shape.

Any Millwall fans curious about the progress of the new stadium will have seen the patch of green space at Senegal Fields turn into a muddy wasteland over recent months but now it was starting to resemble a football ground with stands starting to appear.

It was a constant reminder to them that Millwall's days at The Den were numbered.

After The Lord Mayor's Show

After The Lord Mayor's Show

10

Lions' Feast - and Famine

◇◇◇◇◇◇◇◇◇◇◇◇◇◇◇◇◇◇◇◇◇◇◇◇◇◇◇◇◇

When Millwall travelled to Notts County for their first match of 1993, the countdown to leaving The Den had really kicked into gear. In exactly four months the final league game of the season at home to Bristol Rovers would be the final time their beloved old ground hosted football. Or would it?

Millwall were nestled nicely in the play-off places but were also now level on points with West Ham who occupied the second automatic promotion place. A place in that end-of-season lottery would mean extending their season by at least two games - one of them of course at home.

All the plans were in place for that final day, a release of hundreds of blue and white balloons, former playing legends being paraded around the pitch perimeter to shake fans' hands, and there was also the unplanned, but fairly inevitable prospect that fans would want to go onto the pitch one last time and collect mementoes of their last day at The Den.

All that would have to be put on hold if the Bristol Rovers match turned out to be the penultimate home game of Millwall's season. On one hand, a victorious play-off semi-final and joint celebration of making it to Wembley for a shot at The Premier League coupled with saying a fond farewell to The Den would be a fantastic way to go out. Even if the first leg was at home it would still be a great way to end their 83-year stay at the famously infamous old ground. But one thing must have been playing on the minds of the Millwall board and everyone responsible for organising the day: There was a very real possibility that Millwall's play-off semi-final opponents could be West Ham, and how that would affect any farewell celebrations posed a myriad of headaches.

It wouldn't have been an issue that Mick McCarthy would have allowed to permeate his dressing room. The rookie manager was proving to be a perfect fit for Millwall and he had quickly fixed almost all of the inconsistencies that had plagued the team under its previous administration. His confidence in his ability and that of his team was clear for all fans to see. They were no longer a vulnerable soft-touch when going behind as they had been under Rioch and that was never more in evidence than at Notts County when, despite trailing at half time to a 21st minute Thomas goal, that man Moralee was there again just after half time to level things up and Goodman sealed a winning start to the year with a goal five minutes from time.

London television viewers were noticing some changes too. Thames TV had ceased broadcasting at the end of 1992, and along with it TV-AM and the ITV teletext service Oracle. They would be replaced by Carlton TV, GMTV and the imaginatively named Teletext. The iconic Thames Television ident of the famous London skyline appearing reflected in the river was no more, as would be, in a few months time, The Den. It was a time for change, for revolution.

McCarthy's coaching revolution - his diamond system - had really come into its own and the flexibility of it was underlined when Ian Bogie was able to come in to replace Malcolm Allen almost seamlessly.

The FA Cup draw had produced a fascinating match-up between the two Crystal Palace strikers involved in the Chris Armstrong deal. Millwall travelled to Southend with Jamie Moralee in fine form and his nine goals in fourteen matches since his debut was comparable to another young striker catching the eye in the division: Stan Collymore.

An out-of-sorts Millwall dominated the game but couldn't convert their chances. They failed to score for only the second match in fifteen and it was Collymore who stole the headlines with the only goal. McCarthy refused to lose any sleep over his side's FA Cup campaign ending at the first hurdle - or whether he had signed the right striker from Palace. One thing that was concerning him however was the return of the ugly side of Millwall which reared its head at Southend when some fans invaded the pitch. McCarthy felt that the referee had cut the match short because of the disturbance and denied his side a chance of an equaliser. In his programme notes before the next league match against Brentford, he showed, for the first time, his exasperation at the risk of all the good work being done at the club undone by the actions of a few fans.

The press of course blew it out of proportion compared to a similar incident happening at another club, but that was no excuse, and didn't help McCarthy.

Brian Moore was back at The Den to witness a masterclass in finishing in front of The London

Match cameras. In the first minute Alex Rae weaved his way to the edge of the Brentford penalty area and lashed home The Lions' opener and it was one-way traffic from there.

A 26th minute Phil Barber short corner to Dawes was crossed for Cooper to head the second and it was 3-0 at the break when another brilliant run from Rae left Goodman with the easiest of chances to tap home.

The slaughter resumed immediately after the break and Millwall were playing some of the best football fans had seen in some years. Goodman's pace was terrifying the hapless Bees' back line and it was another of his surging runs that saw him tap the ball past the oncoming 'keeper and Moralee showed the same striker's instinct seen in Teddy Sheringham two seasons before when he smashed home a ball that was already on its way into the net.

At the end of his record-breaking 38-goal season, Sheringham explained how first team coach Steve Harrison had told him to be greedy; to take all the free kicks, penalties and even tap-ins that were already going in from the boot of a teammate. Whilst Moralee was some way behind Teddy of course, he was showing some encouraging signs that he could be the ideal replacement. Brentford pulled a goal back through Gary Blissett but it was only a temporary reprieve as further goals from Moralee and Goodman put the gloss on a crushing 6-1 victory. Millwall were really on a roll now and followed that up with a 4-0 win at home to Peterborough with Tony McCarthy making a goalscoring debut. Barber had scored the first and second half strikes from Goodman and Rae finished Posh off to send them up to third place.

Just as McCarthy's Lions looked ready to pounce on that automatic second place for promotion, they suffered a relapse of their old inconsistencies against the struggling teams in the division.

What should have been a routine three points away to lowly Oxford ended with a stinging 3-0 defeat and allowed West Ham to open up a three point lead in second place:

Barclays League Division One - January 30th 1993

	P	W	D	L	F	A	PTS
1. Newcastle Utd	28	19	5	4	52	24	62
2. West Ham	27	15	6	6	51	26	51
3. MILLWALL	**27**	**13**	**9**	**5**	**47**	**25**	**48**
4. Tranmere	25	13	6	6	49	33	45
5. Portsmouth	27	12	8	7	46	31	44
6. Leicester	27	12	6	9	39	34	42

It was famine or feast now and McCarthy's men showed their lethal home streak once more with another big win in their next match. Moralee, Rae, Cooper and Goodman had them 4-0 up against Watford in 35 remarkable first half minutes and Moralee added a fifth soon after the break. The match finished 5-2 but the defence was back to its miserly best with a goalless draw away to Birmingham to keep a tight grip on third place and stay on West Ham's heels.

The showdown at Upton Park at the end of March was looming on the horizon and could well decide which of the two fierce rivals would ultimately finish in second place. In order to make that happen, Millwall would need to be at their attacking best and defensively sound for the eight games that led up to it. So what happened next was nothing short of disastrous.

A timid 3-0 defeat at play-off hopefuls Swindon was the fourth consecutive away match without scoring and whilst McCarthy seemed to have fixed Millwall's stage fright at The Den, the impressive away form they had shown previously appeared to have deserted them. Relying on home wins to paper over the cracks is often a risky business and so it proved when Millwall hoped to atone for wilting in Wiltshire by battering Barnsley. What actually happened was that the Yorkshire side picked them off at will, capitalising on one schoolboy error after another. Mel Machin's men stormed into a 2-0 lead inside the opening ten minutes and the rampant Wayne Biggins made it three just before the break with his second of the match. Owen Archdeacon bagged his second and Barnsley's fourth thirteen minutes from time to bring The Lions unbeaten home record to an end in stunning style.

McCarthy was now facing his first major challenge as manager and it had come at a crucial time for his team. Whether his diamond formation had been found out or nerves had set in with the home straight in sight wasn't clear.

They managed to break their away goalscoring duck with a 1-1 draw at Cambridge but another blank was drawn in a 0-0 at home to Sunderland and they had now slipped down to fifth place with the gap between them and second place West Ham opened up to seven points.

What was most frustrating about this latest little barren spell was that it had once again come against teams at the opposite end of the table. Birmingham looked doomed to relegation while Barnsley, Sunderland and Cambridge were experiencing erratic form and nervously looking over the shoulders at the bottom three.

In typically unshakeable fashion though, McCarthy refused to panic and regrouped his troops to get back to winning ways with a 1-0 win at Bristol City courtesy of Phil Barber. Their luck really seemed to have changed for the better in the next match at home to Derby when they were awarded a penalty in the third minute of injury time which Malcolm Allen duly despatched to make it two in two.

Stan Collymore looked to be haunting Millwall again as they returned to Roots Hall and found themselves a goal behind to the ex-Palace man after twelve minutes but goals from Barber, Stevens and Goodman in the last ten minutes of the first half turned the match on its head and sent McCarthy's men in at half time with a commanding 3-1 lead and looking good for three wins on the spin.

The warning signs were there early in the second half however when Tilson made it 3-2 and there was a certain inevitability about it when he scored his second and Southend's equaliser with just three minutes left.

It was a hammer blow for Millwall, looking to go into their crucial trip to West Ham seven days later with as much momentum as possible, and even a return to winning ways with a Moralee-inspired 1-0 at home to Luton before the short trip east of the capital couldn't erase the self-doubt that was creeping into The Lions' once-impregnable back line.

The London Match cameras were present again as Millwall faced West Ham in fifth place, five points and three places behind their rivals. A win was vital if they were to have any chance of stealing that second automatic place. A draw - which eight games ago would have been useful when the sides were level on points - would be of little use. Defeat was unthinkable. What Millwall needed was to hit West Ham early and that's exactly what happened.

There was less than sixty seconds on the clock when Malcolm Allen received the ball on the edge of the centre circle inside West Ham's half. He turned to his left where Moralee had made another of his instinctive runs between two home defenders and Allen's ball was inch-perfect.

Moralee's pace and perfectly timed run took him into the Hammers' penalty area and he poked home the opener before hurling himself into the delirious Lions fans behind the goal.

Unfortunately, such was Millwall's fragility when in the lead by now, when Keen levelled on thirteen minutes panic set in and before they even had chance to settle, Morley made it 2-1 to Billy Bonds' side straight from the restart. The Lions were in trouble. They steadied the ship and a Keith Stevens equaliser with just over ten minutes remaining gave them hope, but the match finished 2-2 and chances of a top two place were all but gone. What made it worse was Portsmouth and Swindon had now played their way into the reckoning and overtaken Millwall, making that 3-0 defeat at The County Ground look all the more damaging, and the upcoming Easter Saturday visit of Pompey to The Den absolutely crucial:

Barclays League Division One - March 27th 1993

	P	W	D	L	F	A	PTS
1. Newcastle Utd	38	22	9	7	69	34	75
2. West Ham	38	20	10	8	65	35	70
3. Portsmouth	38	20	9	9	64	39	69
4. Swindon	38	18	11	9	62	46	65
5. MILLWALL	**38**	**17**	**14**	**7**	**61**	**40**	**65**
6. Leicester	37	19	7	11	60	48	64

The match came after the traditional end-of-March transfer deadline and McCarthy had dived into the market to make three signings - all of whom raised an eyebrow or two. Tommy Gaynor arrived from Nottingham Forest, tough defender Gavin McGuire signed from that day's visitors Portsmouth with the fee due to be set by tribunal and Danny Wallace on loan from Manchester United.

The signings were intended to add some extra experience going into the home straight of the season - and the now almost inevitable play-off campaign - but they were also needed to alleviate another injury crisis that was hampering McCarthy's efforts to take a settled starting eleven into the most crucial period of the campaign. McGuire made his Millwall bow coming on as a substitute in the draw at West Ham and started against his former club alongside Tony McCarthy in a reshuffled Millwall defence. It was a pairing that took time to settle and the signs were ominous as a Mark Chamberlain goal just before half time gave Pompey the advantage.

Also making his Lions debut from the bench at West Ham was Canadian striker John Kerr who had been brought in on a trial basis. McCarthy introduced him to the action again when he replaced Malcolm Allen in the 56th minute and his impact was almost immediate, hitting the equaliser less than ten minutes after coming on. The draw was of more use to Portsmouth than Millwall though and it was about to get worse when The Lions travelled to Grimsby three days later, going down 1-0 to a last minute Clive Mendonca penalty. Millwall's miserable run since that thumping 5-2 victory over Watford had produced just 14 points from a possible 36 and seen them reduced from genuine top two contenders to a side devoid of confidence and clinging on to that last play-off spot by their fingernails. What heaped even more pressure on them was that their last six games saw them face two teams looking to nick that sixth place in Tranmere and Leicester and champions-elect Newcastle. Millwall had to start winning again.

While the first team were losing at Grimsby, Tom Whalley's talented youth squad was once again making progress in the FA Youth Cup. In the first leg at Old Trafford, goals from Neville Gordon and Mark Kennedy gave The Lions a stunning 2-1 win against a United side that was already being lauded as a team of the future.

Tranmere visited The Den with only an outside chance of overhauling The Lions, being five points behind but having a game in hand. If Millwall could defeat the Wirral outfit that would surely see off that particular threat and reduce it down to a straight two-way fight between them and Leicester.

Tranmere were clearly happy to settle for a single point and frustrated Millwall throughout the match where The Lions never looked like making the breakthrough in a dour goalless display. Things started more brightly away to Leicester however but once again that final killer touch was missing as an opening thirty minutes of dominance failed to produce a Millwall goal.

Disaster then struck when Leicester were awarded what looked like a dubious free kick which Agnew scored in the 34th minute and a cruel deflection following a shot from Thompson soon after the break made it two. Oldfield gave the game a somewhat unfairly one-sided look at

3-0 and suddenly Millwall were outside the top six for the first time in almost six months.

There had been more disappointment 24 hours earlier when a healthy crowd of almost 7,000 turned up at The Den hoping to see Millwall's youth team compete their semi-final win over Manchester United. But they were unable to prevent United from overturning that fantastic first leg advantage and, after a 2-0 defeat, went out of the competition 3-2 on aggregate.

Tranmere had won their game in hand and that victory, while Millwall were losing at Leicester, saw them leapfrog The Lions. After being in the driving seat for so long they were playing catch-up with matches quickly running out. Millwall's dream of moving into their new stadium as a Premier League club was quickly turning into a nightmare and with Kevin Keegan's Newcastle the next visitors to The Den, it was going to take a superhuman effort just to nick that final play-of spot from Tranmere.

Phil Barber gave Lions fans hope when he gave them the lead midway through the first half and it was a lead they maintained at the break but which looked precarious against a Newcastle side full of goals. It was to prove the case as goals from Lee Clark and Andy Cole turned the match around for the visitors. With Tranmere winning again there was now a gap of four points between the two teams with just three matches remaining and Tranmere having played a game less.

Portsmouth's incredible run had now seen them overtake West Ham in second place and if Millwall were to achieve the unlikely feat of clawing back those four points and snatching sixth place from Tranmere, the prospect of West Ham providing the last ever opposition for Millwall at The Den in a play-off semi-final first leg was now a very realistic one.

A goal from Goodman was enough to give Millwall a 1-0 home victory over Charlton - just their second in nine attempts - but a first half horror show away to Wolves where they found themselves 3-0 down by the break signalled the end of their season.

Millwall's fans were shellshocked. In just a few matches they had watched teams fly past them like speeding cars overtaking them on a motorway with The Lions floundering on the hard shoulder. Even when points were being squandered, they had still somehow found themselves in sixth place with a cushion over those below them.

But with the likes of Leicester and Tranmere hitting form at just the right time and Millwall saving their worst for the crucial run-in, that cushion soon evaporated and before they could do anything about it their chance was gone.

Now all that was left to do was shake off the disappointment and give their famous old ground the send-off it deserved.

11

Den End Game

◇◇◇◇◇◇◇◇◇◇◇◇◇◇◇◇◇◇◇◇◇◇◇◇◇◇◇◇◇◇

It wasn't the send-off they were hoping for. The omens were good. Almost exactly five years to the day since The Den had hosted the biggest party ever seen in south London to celebrate promotion to the First Division, it should have been hosting a farewell knees-up to put even that in the shade.

It wasn't to be of course. Hardened, long-suffering Millwall supporters will not have been surprised. Rarely are there happy endings at The Den and even promotion to the new Premier League at the expense of West Ham would have been tinged with the sadness of the famous old ground not being able to host more top flight football. At least now they could wallow completely in the sadness of it all. No promotion. No play-offs and, after today, no more Den. Most of the division's business had been concluded

- but there were a couple of issues still to be settled on the final day - including West Ham's automatic promotion. Portsmouth had matched them all the way to the final hurdle and were in third place behind The Hammers only by virtue of goal difference. If Millwall fans couldn't sweeten the sadness of leaving their home, at least they might have schadenfreude in the shape of West Ham missing out at the end of an emotional afternoon. They would, but not in the way they would have expected. The contrast between the damp disappointment of a drizzly Den day to welcome Bristol Rovers as the final opponents at their home of 83 years and the sun-drenched celebrations of five years before to mark promotion to the top flight against Blackburn Rovers was stark.

Fans lapped up the parading of former heroes such as Kitchener and Cripps and a specially produced programme beautifully depicted eight decades of footballing drama, huge highs and devastating lows, all played out against the unmistakable and inimitable backdrop of The Den. It was real lump-in-the-throat stuff.

The match understandably became a similar anti-climax to the promotion party of five years before when Millwall had already clinched the title and Blackburn were striving for a final push into the play-offs. On this occasion, already relegated Bristol Rovers, who had managed just nine wins all season and were ten points adrift at the bottom of the table, also had nothing to play for but made it ten and complete the double with a 3-0 victory that summed up Millwall's season.

On the final whistle fans flooded the pitch and started to collect mementoes which ranged from players' clothing to lumps of Den turf. While it had very much been a dead rubber day at The Den, elsewhere there was high drama. West Ham clinched their place in the top two - but they were made to work for it. Pompey did their bit by beating Grimsby 2-1 but West Ham just made it over the line with a 2-0 win at home to Cambridge. It was a defeat which sent Cambridge down and they were joined by Brentford.

There was some cause for celebration for Millwall fans however. The first ever Premier League season was reaching a similarly dramatic climax in its relegation battle. Oldham were in a straight two-way scrap with Crystal Palace for the last place but even though they led Southampton 4-1 on the final day, they needed Palace to lose at Arsenal to save them. With points level and goal difference close, it was going to go right to the wire and as Southampton whittled away the deficit from three goals to just one, Palace could afford to lose 1-0 at Highbury and still stay up. But Arsenal added two more and at the final whistle it was Crystal Palace that occupied the final relegation place of the first Premier League season with a record high amount of points for a relegated top flight team.

The result and confirmation of Palace's demise was broadcast over the PA at The Den, prompting a conga across the pitch which now resembled a ploughed field.

Portsmouth were unable to continue their end-of-season surge through the play-offs and lost out to Leicester in their semi-final. Swindon defeated Tranmere in their match and won a thrilling Wembley final 4-3 against Leicester to claim a place in the top flight for the first time in their history. It came three years after they had won a play-off final against Sunderland to the top flight but had their promotion withdrawn following financial irregularities. Soon after their win, manager Glenn Hoddle joined Chelsea.

For Millwall another season had ended in disappointment and left their fans with a summer of "what-ifs" to ponder. They had fallen just six points short in the end. Six points that were squandered in the final two, extremely winnable games against Wolves and Bristol Rovers. With a superior goal difference to Leicester, a win by any means in both would have seen them face Portsmouth in a play-off semi final and another golden chance to appear in the Wembley showpiece and claim a place in the Premier League.

It was a Premier League that had been won in its first season by Manchester United, giving Alex Ferguson's side their first top flight title in 26 years. It was a league that Millwall were now desperate to be a part of. Once again they had come so close, only to fall close to the finish line.

Now they would have to try again. This time in a new stadium and with new backers. The club had signed its first ever fully commercial shirt sponsorship deal with a recognised brand.

In their shiny new stadium they'd certainly be talking the talk, but could they walk the walk?

Barclays League Division One 1992-93 Final Table

Newcastle United	**46**	**29**	**9**	**8**	**92**	**38**	**+54**	**96**	**Champions**
West Ham United	**46**	**26**	**10**	**10**	**81**	**41**	**+40**	**88**	**Promoted**
Portsmouth	**46**	**26**	**10**	**10**	**80**	**46**	**+34**	**88**	
Tranmere Rovers	**46**	**23**	**10**	**13**	**72**	**56**	**+16**	**79**	
Swindon Town	**46**	**21**	**13**	**12**	**74**	**59**	**+15**	**76**	**Play-off winners**
Leicester City	**46**	**22**	**10**	**14**	**71**	**64**	**+7**	**76**	
Millwall	46	18	16	12	65	53	+12	70	
Derby County	46	19	9	18	68	57	+11	66	
Grimsby Town	46	19	7	20	58	57	+1	64	
Peterborough	46	16	14	16	55	63	–8	62	
Wolves	46	16	13	17	57	56	+1	61	
Charlton	46	16	13	17	49	46	+3	61	
Barnsley	46	17	9	20	56	60	–4	60	
Oxford United	46	14	14	18	53	56	–3	56	
Bristol City	46	14	14	18	49	67	–18	56	
Watford	46	14	13	19	57	71	–14	55	
Notts County	46	12	16	18	55	70	–15	52	
Southend United	46	13	13	20	54	64	–10	52	
Birmingham City	46	13	12	21	50	72	–22	51	
Luton Town	46	10	21	15	48	62	–14	51	
Sunderland	46	13	11	22	50	64	–14	50	
Brentford	**46**	**13**	**10**	**23**	**52**	**71**	**–19**	**49**	
Cambridge United	**46**	**11**	**16**	**19**	**48**	**69**	**–21**	**49**	
Bristol Rovers	**46**	**10**	**11**	**25**	**55**	**87**	**–32**	**41**	

93/94

a rum do

12

Culture Shock

◇◇◇◇◇◇◇◇◇◇◇◇◇◇◇◇◇◇◇◇◇◇◇◇◇◇◇◇◇

When The New Den opened its doors for the first time it was like walking into a surreal new world. Everything was shiny, new, pristine, perfect. It didn't really fit in with what Millwall fans had been used to at all. It was like The Artful Dodger had been given a scrub-up and makeover with a brand new suit and shoes.

Whilst it felt a little odd and uncomfortable initially, when the ribbon was cut to officially declare the stadium open by The Rt Hon John Smith MP, leader of the Labour Party and the first referee's whistle blown to start the first match, it started to feel a little better.

The opposition for this historic occasion was Sporting Lisbon. They had been brought to this little corner of south London by their manager Bobby Robson - which in itself went a little way to slaying a few ghosts. The last time Robson had brought a team to face Millwall was on that infamous Saturday in March 1978 when his Ipswich side swept them aside 6-1 in an FA Cup quarter final.

In a match constantly delayed by crowd disturbance where Robson was apparently confronted and verbally abused, he made no secret of his contempt for those that had marred the day, recommending the authorities 'Set the flame-throwers on them.' Maybe this was now a time for Millwall and Robson to make their peace. The match was an entertaining 2-1 victory for the Portuguese giants, their goals coming somewhat charitably after John Kerr had been afforded the historic honour of scoring the first ever goal at the new ground.

It wasn't just the ground that was shiny and new of course. Millwall's players were sporting a new kit, and for the first time, anyone looking at the logo emblazoned on its front didn't need to ask: "Who's that?"

Leading drinks brand Captain Morgan had shaken hands on a deal and taken the plunge where so many globally recognised brands had shied away. Millwall had worked tirelessly to try and secure the kind of lucrative shirt sponsorship deals that their rivals were enjoying but without any success which was slowly but surely pushing them further behind them. Finally, the move to a brand new stadium had, it seemed, helped to show that Millwall was shaking off the shackles of its dirty old image and entering a brave new world with a clean slate. They were going places and finally, others wanted to come with them.

The large glossy programme produced to commemorate that first match was packed with features and statistics about their shiny new state-of-the-art arena. It was all so un-Millwall like. Executive boxes, plush conferencing and dining, computerised ticket offices with dozens of windows to serve fans and, a description that regular old Den-goers would have found amusing: 'open-plan club shop'. For supporters used to years of visiting the old place and tapping on Billy Neil's window to retrieve tickets through the bars of his window or edging their way around the cosy concrete cavern that passed as a place to buy their merchandise and programmes this was indeed a brave new world.

For any fans cynical about Millwall's boasts of leading the way in such developments, they only had to read the message from John Sinigaglia, the new 'stadium director' and chief of Ogden Entertainments, the American company that had been brought in to maximise the revenue potential of this new venture. Ogden were, as Sinigaglia explained, the world's largest venue management company, handling events for such sporting behemoths as the LA Lakers. One term that he used early on in the piece might have raised some consternation among Lions fans.

He referred to it as 'The New London Stadium', a moniker reinforced on the front page of the programme. Was this the end of The Den? Fans had been promised that this was a reboot of their beloved home and the legendary name at least would live on if the old bricks and mortar had to be demolished.

Sinigaglia continued to explain how all of the world's top concert promoters had been to the venue and the plan was to host a huge variety of world-renowned artists and events. Some slightly sceptical fans will have muttered a very audible "Believe it when I see it" having read that line.

Even more cynical supporters will have certainly turned their noses up with the appearance, at Ogden's behest, of "The Crown Jewels", the cheerleaders for the London Monarchs American Football team and the promise of an 'unusual musical treat' before the next pre-season opener against Hungarian side Honved.

This was supposed to be Millwall. They didn't

do glitz and glamour; they didn't do cheerleaders, musical sideshows or extra large buckets of Coke and foot-long hot dogs. They wanted a pie and a beer. Most of all, they wanted a winning football team.

Summer transfer activity had of course been overshadowed by the big move-in, and it was just as well because as far as most Lions fans were concerned, it didn't make pretty reading.

Colin Cooper had become one of the leading defenders outside the top flight since McCarthy converted him from his original left-back position to a more central role. It was an accolade confirmed by his naming in the First Division Select XI for the 92/93 season. Millwall fans were expecting him to be the lynchpin of their challenge for a place in the Premier League, but he was sold to Nottingham Forest for £1.75m before a ball had even been kicked.

Explained as, like the Chris Armstrong deal, being an offer to good to refuse, it was clear to supporters that it was far more likely a case of a final payment due for the new ground. Disgruntled fans were still struggling to get their heads around the necessity to move in order to realistically achieve and retain top flight football, when it felt they were selling off the very players that were needed to get them there. It was a familiar catch 22 situation, and not just for Millwall.

Transfers in to the club were pretty unremarkable. Defenders James Saddington and Richard Huxford arrived from Cambridge City and Barnet respectively and winger Lee Luscombe was signed from under the noses of West Ham thanks to a postal delay. The Brentford wide man looked set for the Premier League with the newly promoted Hammers but after a hold-up in getting his registration finalised, Millwall took the opportunity to nab him.

Also joining was American striker Bruce Murray. Footballers from the other side of the pond have always been welcomed with a slight air of suspicion and Murray's footballing CV wasn't glowing to say the least.

After leaving Maryland Bays when the collapse of the American Professional Soccer League was imminent, he signed a contract with the U.S. Soccer Federation (USSF) to play full-time with the U.S. national team before being released to explore professional football opportunities in Europe.

After joining Millwall for their pre-season tour of Ireland and featuring in The Lions' other summer warm-up matches, he signed on the dotted line following the final friendly at home to Honved and was given an immediate start in the first match of the season at Stoke. And what a start it was.

After The Lord Mayor's Show

13

There's No Place Like Home

◇◇◇◇◇◇◇◇◇◇◇◇◇◇◇◇◇◇◇◇◇◇◇◇◇◇◇◇◇◇

Mick McCarthy's starting line-up for the season opener had a blend of youth and experience with a trans-Atlantic twist. Murray joined Canadian Kerr in the Millwall frontline and a defence of Cunningham, Dawes, McGuire and Tony McCarthy in front of American 'keeper Keller.

The midfield saw a return to the side for Keith Stevens after an injury lay-off the previous season and he was joined by Ian Bogie and youngsters Andy Roberts and Tony Dolby. There had been another shock departure on the eve of the match though when Malcolm Allen signed for newly promoted Newcastle, leaving the side worryingly short of quality in many fans' eyes but with McCarthy fighting fires on two fronts - with a squad too big for the club's resources and a growing injury list - there was a delicate balancing act to perform.

It was, some supporters felt, a more disjointed and less balanced side than had looked so good during the purple patch of the previous season, but when Bogie finally scored his first goal for the club on fourteen minutes, those that had made the journey to the potteries were happy to give it the benefit of the doubt.

Even when Stoke equalised through a rather unfortunate McCarthy own goal (something that seemed to be a right of passage for Millwall defenders of that name) they were encouraged by the trouble both Murray and Kerr were causing the Stoke defence.

Murray's graft was rewarded just after the hour when he struck what turned out to be the winner and confidence was high among fans for the visit of Southend for the first ever league match at the new stadium. Southend, like Millwall, had sold one of their star players to Nottingham Forest that summer and The Lions' back four would no doubt have been grateful not to have to face the pacey Stan Collymore who had been a thorne in their side in previous meetings.

Fans among the somewhat disappointing crowd of just over 10,000 would have been doubly delighted to see the other half of Millwall's new-look striking partnership get on the scoresheet when John Kerr gave his side the lead midway through the first half. There was hope that two defeats in the opening two matches of the new stadium against Sporting Lisbon and Honved were out of the system and the home league campaign would start with a win. That hope lasted less than thirty minutes and by the time referee Keren Barratt blew his whistle to bring the first league match at The New Den to an end, many fans had already vacated their shiny new seats after witnessing their side taken apart 4-1 by a youthful, pacey and incisive Southend.

Worse was to follow with two away trips to the midlands in quick succession resulting in a 2-0 defeat at Wolves and a 4-0 thrashing to Leicester. Fans that bothered to turn up for the next home match with Charlton in the Anglo Italian Cup must have been dreading a humiliating fourth successive loss in their new home against their rivals.

Relief at taking what seemed like an unassailable lead through first half goals from Andy Roberts and the fit-again Etienne Verveer was soon replaced with disbelief as Charlton were allowed back into the game to level through Leaburn and Grant. It may have only been September but already Millwall were rock bottom and fans were starting to wonder if there was a need for a 10,000-seater stadium let alone one with a capacity of twice that number. Just over 8,000 turned up hoping that Barnsley wouldn't inflict more humiliation and were rewarded by another Kerr goal and a second from the returning Alex Rae to cap a 2-0 victory and finally notch up their first win at their new home in five attempts.

A goalless draw at early season leaders Charlton saw the debut of veteran defender Pat Van Den Hauwe alongside Keith Stevens in the centre of Millwall's defence - a frightening proposition for any striker.

Van Den Hauwe had actually grown up close to The Den and gone to school with Dave Mehmet - who had progressed through the ranks in the 1970s and become a regular in the Millwall first team from the age of 16 - but his career had taken him on a much more exotic path via international football for Belgium, and English league title, cup and European glory with Everton.

Van Den Hauwe's experience seemed to do the trick and - aside from a meaningless 3-0 defeat to Crystal Palace in the utterly ridiculous Anglo Italian Cup that no team wanted to play in - Millwall made it five clean sheets in a row. Unfortunately they were unable to score in four of them, producing a string of goalless draws against Derby, Watford and Peterborough to add to the one at Charlton.

While goalkeepers were not seeing much action in Millwall's matches, there was no lack of incident elsewhere. The encouraging positive of Millwall's new stadium hosting its first England international for the under 21 match against Poland was overshadowed by more idiocy and overreaction from the nation's gutter press.

A recent local election had seen the right wing British National Party win a by-election in Tower Hamlets. Never ones to let the facts get in the way of a story, The Sun ran a piece in their column by Steve Howard which ludicrously linked Millwall Football Club to the party's victory. Even by the paper's usually lazy, ill-informed journalistic standards, this was a particularly pathetic piece that received rebuke from both McCarthy and Reg Burr. Howard's column, dubiously billed as 'a must for players and fans alike' took a swipe at the Millwall chief before dropping his embarrassing geographical gaffe:

"Not long ago chairman Reg Burr claimed racism has all been all but eliminated from Millwall. How odd then that the facist British National Party should have won its first seat in Tower Hamlets last week. In the Millwall ward."
What was of course completely lost on empty-headed Howard was that Millwall Football Club

hadn't played at Millwall for over 80 years.

A brilliant piece in the club programme calling out the joke publication's shameful article was backed up by a fierce fightback from McCarthy in his manager's notes and a typically eloquent piece by chairman Burr. Sadly of course, the damage had already been done and incorrect facts planted in the minds of readers that didn't know any different.

The Watford draw had come away in a League Cup first leg. The Lions would then face The Hornets in successive matches at The Den with the league match following on from the second leg. It would prove to be an end to Millwall's goal drought, and provide an a bit of unexpected post-match entertainment for some fans too.

Jon Goodman celebrated his first Millwall hat-trick in a 4-1 win to extend the unbeaten league run to five and four days later the two sides shared seven goals in a thrilling League Cup second leg class. Watford stormed into a 2-0 lead before goals from Huxford and Murray made it 2-2 at the break, only for Hessenthaler to restore the visitors' lead on the hour mark.

A Moralee goal took the tie to extra time and as tempers boiled over Etienne Verveer hit the winner in the final minutes as penalties beckoned.

The fun and games didn't end there though. As the Millwall Clubcall telephone service recorded their post-match interview with Lions' goalscorer Bruce Murray in the tunnel, they were interrupted by an irate Glenn Roeder.

The disappointed Watford boss, still incensed at his side's late loss, made a comment as he passed Murray and, rather than ignore it and continue answering questions, the American striker turned on Roeder and then proceeded to tell Clubcall listeners exactly what he thought of him.

Roeder gave as good as he got and the whole exchange was left in for callers to enjoy. For once, they got good value for their 45p per minute.

Goals from Goodman and Rae made it three home wins on the spin in a 2-1 victory over West Brom but a few old boys returned to haunt them in their next away trip. Bolton had enjoyed far more success with Bruce Rioch at the helm than Millwall after winning promotion as runners up from Division Two.

A big part of that success had been the goals of John McGinlay and the Scottish striker had continued to find the net that season.

With ex-Lion Keith Branagan in goal keeping a clean sheet, McGinlay showed Millwall what they were missing with two goals in a crushing 4-0 win for Bolton. The Lions' away form had once again deserted them and a 1-0 defeat at Birmingham was the ninth consecutive league and cup match on their travels without a goal since Bruce Murray's opening day winner at Stoke.

That terrible run was finally broken with an emphatic win at Nottingham Forest - Cooper and Collymore included - where goals from Goodman, Murray and Stevens earned them a 3-1 triumph.

It was just as well his side had given them that cushion because Mick McCarthy might have paid the price for giving the linesman in front of him some 'friendly advice' earlier in the match when the referee had to withdraw injured and was replaced by, yes, you've guessed it, the official that he had been giving stick to!

Thankfully Millwall were now starting to feel at home in their new surroundings and had not tasted defeat since that dreadful curtain-raiser against Southend.

A 2-0 victory over Notts County was the latest one and saw them make their first appearance of the season in a top six which had a very south London look to it.

There was also the opportunity to put the pressure on the top two automatic promotion places when Middlesbrough arrived at The Den.

Endsleigh League Division One - October 20th 1993							
	P	W	D	L	F	A	PTS
1. Tranmere	12	7	2	3	18	13	23
2. Charlton	12	6	5	1	15	10	23
3. Middlesbrough	12	6	3	3	23	14	21
4. Crystal Palace	10	6	3	1	21	8	21
5. Leicester	10	6	1	3	17	11	19
6. MILLWALL	**12**	**5**	**3**	**4**	**13**	**17**	**18**

A solid 1-1 draw against the promotion-chasing Teessiders saw the debut of an exciting youngster who fans had already been regularly reading about in recent editions of the programme.

Mark Kennedy had earned himself a fearsome reputation coming through the ranks as a prolific goalscorer and, despite still only being 17, was blessed with a physical strength way beyond his young years.

He certainly didn't look out of place and there was little surprise when, in just his fifth start, he hit two brilliant goals in a home 2-2 draw with Oxford. On target for the visitors that day was John Byrne who had joined the Us from Millwall after a spell on loan at former club Brighton. Byrne had mysteriously been unable to produce the goalscoring form at The Den that he had enjoyed at Brighton and Sunderland previously with just a solitary strike to show for 17 Lions appearances. Typically he would need less than an hour of his Oxford debut to score against

Millwall and would go on to return a decent 11 goals in all competitions for the club that season.

There was a certain amount of disgruntlement at McCarthy's decision to substitute Kennedy soon after Oxford's second equaliser and fans that travelled to Bristol City for the next match (where goals from Goodman and Beard saw them come back from 0-2 down to snatch a draw) were dumbfounded to see that he had been relegated to a place on the bench.

It was easy to forget however that Kennedy was still only 17 and needed protecting. McCarthy treated the reaction with typical wit in his programme notes for the visit of Tranmere:

"No doubt I'll be criticised for leaving Mark Kennedy on the bench at Bristol City after his two goals against Oxford, and I can assure you I just did it to annoy people and upset Mark!"

The truth was, with the injury list finally starting to shorten and another new arrival to bolster his attacking options, McCarthy could afford to shuffle his pack and wrap Millwall's latest young star in cotton wool.

The Lions international roll call had now added Australia to its ranks with the addition of striker Dave Mitchell. The former Swindon man had frequently been a thorn in the side when facing them for the Wiltshire club and made his bow as a substitute in the defeat at Bolton. It wasn't long before he found the net when he gave Millwall an eighth minute lead against second-place Tranmere and Goodman quickly made it two. Kennedy was back in the starting line-up now, being played in a more unfamiliar wide role but still managing to find the net again to give The Lions an impressive 3-1 over the promotion chasing Wirral side.

The bearded Mitchell, who quickly earned the nickname 'Beadle' from the club's excellent fanzine The Lion Roars, after the popular television practical joker, was about again for the next game when he scored the only goal in a 1-0 home victory over Grimsby.

There was another welcome return from the physio's bench in Etienne Verveer and he celebrated with a late winner at Oxford to extend Millwall's unbeaten run to six, with three wins in a row and a place in the top six.

That was quickly five in a row and a lofty third place thanks to a win at Notts County and at home to Stoke. The Notts County victory was particularly impressive. Having fallen behind to a Lund goal immediately after half time, and still trailing with 25 minutes to go, Millwall looked to be heading for an undeserved defeat in a match they had dominated but failed to find the net.

Enter Alex Rae who sent the travelling fans wild with a stunning 17-minute hat-trick that blew County away.

Even when teams tried to park the bus they found Millwall both patient - and lethal - as Stoke discovered when they thought they had held out for a Christmas point at The Den. Goals from Rae and Kennedy in the last three minutes sent The Lions into the final home game of the year at home to sixth-placed Portsmouth in third place, just a point behind leaders Crystal Palace and second placed Tranmere, with Palace next to visit The Den on New Year's Day.

For once, Millwall were unable to break down a resolute defence as Pompey held out for a 0-0 Den draw. With Palace winning and Tranmere also picking up a point it meant that top spot was frustratingly out of reach for McCarthy's men in what was the first match they had failed to find the net in two months.

More exasperation was to follow when the fixture computer ludicrously decided to send them on the long journey north east to Sunderland just 24 hours later and despite Andy Roberts cancelling out Gray's opener, Russell's winner inflicted Millwall's first defeat in ten at the hands of the struggling Wearsiders. Palace meanwhile had an extra day to recover from their short trip to

Oxford and prepare for their home match against Southend where they picked up their fourth win in a row to extend their lead at the summit.

Tranmere, who also had an extra 24 hours rest, secured another draw to remain in second place as the year ended on a slightly disappointing note. Millwall had now slipped back to fourth, a point behind Charlton, two off Tranmere and six adrift of Palace. All they could do was try and reduce that to three when The Eagles visited The Den for the first match of 1994.

It was a first London derby for league points at the new stadium, and it would need a big performance from McCarthy's men to keep apace with the top two and send out a statement of intent to the rest of the division. The pressure was on, would The Lions be up to it?

Endsleigh League Division One - December 29th 1993

	P	W	D	L	F	A	PTS
1. Crystal Palace	23	14	4	5	43	24	46
2. Tranmere	24	12	6	6	35	24	42
3. Charlton	23	12	5	6	29	20	41
4. MILLWALL	**24**	**11**	**7**	**6**	**33**	**28**	**40**
5. Leicester	23	10	7	6	38	26	37
6. Southend	23	11	4	8	38	30	37

After The Lord Mayor's Show

14

Old Habits Die Hard

◇◇◇◇◇◇◇◇◇◇◇◇◇◇◇◇◇◇◇◇◇◇◇◇◇◇◇◇◇◇

Crystal Palace had become something of a jinx for Millwall. With the exception of a 3-2 win in an end-of-season dead rubber at The Den in 1986, The Lions had been unable to get the better of The Eagles in the league for almost twenty years.

You had to go back to December 1975 and a 2-1 home win for Gordon Jago's boys in that remarkable season where they pipped their rivals to a promotion place.

Palace arrived at The Den in fine form and one of the favourites to make an immediate return to the Premier League. They had already beaten Millwall 3-0 in an early season Anglo Italian Cup tie where ex-Lion Chris Armstrong was on target. Armstrong had been prolific for Palace so far, already bagging 13 league goals, and McCarthy's prime objective was to keep him quiet. It all went according to plan in a cagey first half which produced little incident in either goalmouth. In the second half Millwall blew away their supporters' hangovers with a performance in front of their new stadium's highest league crowd which finally made it feel like home.

Goodman had the only clear cut chance of the first half when he was played in behind the Palace back four with a beautiful ball from Rae but Nigel Martin turned his shot past the post. He made no mistake with his next opportunity on 51 minutes though and after more good work from Rae who found Verveer inside the box, the tricky Dutch master jinked his way into space before standing up the perfect cross for Goodman to rise above Eric Young and plant a perfect header beyond Martin.

The ET show was complete eight minutes later when an outswinging corner from the left was met on the penalty spot by Mitchell. Attempting to head the ball goalwards, it came off his back and straight into the ground, sitting up perfectly for Verveer who had been waiting on the front post and was now approaching the lose ball in the centre of the six yard box with his back to goal.

Instinctively he flicked the ball over his head and it pinged into the Palace net off the bar. By now the atmosphere being created by almost 17,000 fans in the new arena was electric and arguably rivalling anything the old Den had produced in recent years, if not quite as raw.

Rae, Goodman and Mitchell were terrorising the Palace defence now and just two minutes later Goodman nodded on a Rae header just inside the area to Mitchell who was again positioned on the spot kick mark with Eric Young in close attendance. Mitchell shielded the ball and turned deftly away from the defender and, as he was shaping to shoot, was brought crashing to the turf.

The referee had no hesitation in pointing to the spot and Rae gleefully slotted home Millwall's third to give them their biggest win over Palace in over a quarter of a century. McCarthy's men had now beaten the top two teams at home, scoring three goals in the process and, but for their Christmas blip against Pompey and Sunderland would by now be clear at the top. Somehow they were still in fourth place for the visit of Bruce Rioch's Bolton a fortnight later in what was the third home match in a row.

The previous week, that Palace attendance had been bettered when just over 20,000 filled the new stadium for the visit of Arsenal in the FA Cup third round and George Graham's Gunners were given the fright of their lives, escaping with a fortunate 1-0 win thanks to a last-minute goal from Tony Adams. Back in league action, Bolton arrived with another familiar face in Aidan Davison who was now in goal for Rioch's Wanderers.

Millwall were keen for revenge for that 4-0 defeat at Burnden Park earlier in the season and it came in the shape of a slightly more modest 1-0 thanks to a second half Rae goal. What was more important was that it meant Millwall had finally got themselves into those precious top two automatic promotion slots. It was still only January though and the hard bit would be staying there until May with nineteen matches still to play.

The Lions' downfall had often been their failure to get points against struggling teams and whilst a draw away from home is never a bad thing when going for promotion (if you're following the old formula of win at home, draw away which usually guarantees success) there was some disappointment that they immediately surrendered that second place back to Charlton with a 0-0 draw at fourth-bottom West Brom.

Worse was to follow when they travelled to Middlesbrough who were languishing in 17th place and had won only two of their previous fourteen matches. In a match bizarrely reminiscent of Millwall's first defeat of their inaugural top flight season back in October 1989, 'Boro took a first half lead only for two quick goals before the break sent The Lions in 2-1 ahead. The Teessiders then swamped The Lions in the second period scoring three without reply to replicate that 4-2 defeat and suddenly Millwall were back down to fifth.

Etienne Verveer was really cementing his place as a fan favourite now and his two goals helped to see off Birmingham at The Den next. Dave Mitchell also had a growing fan club and 'Beadle' was on hand to help earn a point at Southend in a match which saw the return of a cult Millwall hero with Terry Hurlock making his second debut for The Lions. McCarthy had been quick to snap the midfielder up after he had been released from Premier League Southampton.

His experience would certainly come in handy, with the season moving into its home straight, the usually jostling of places and surges from teams on the fringes had begun. Like late dashes from contenders in the Grand National, Nottingham Forest, Leicester, Derby and Stoke had emerged seemingly from nowhere with a string of wins and were now making the top six very congested, plunging Millwall into seventh.

Tranmere had inexplicably lost form and fallen

away, and Charlton were starting to wobble, desperately trying to cling on to Palace's coat tails at the top but suddenly with four more teams on their tail.

Millwall faced fourth place Leicester at home and fifth placed Derby away in successive matches, with Charlton arriving at The Den after that. April would then see successive matches against Palace and Forest. Lions fans were starting to have a recurring nightmare of the previous season when first a likely promotion and then expected play-off place disintegrated in a tricky end-of-season run-in.

Did they have the nerve for it this time?

During his first spell at Millwall, Terry Hurlock lasted eight matches before receiving his first red card for the club. In this, his second home debut, he managed eight minutes. Keen to announce his return, a moment of madness saw The Lions reduced to ten men with most of the game to play against a very good Leicester side which meant a goalless draw was probably the best they could have hoped for.

That scoreline was repeated away to Derby, although by now Millwall had managed to leapfrog The Rams into fifth place, which perfectly set up the next match: fourth placed Charlton at home. The Lions battered their local rivals in a first half which should have seen them at least three goals to the good with two brilliant efforts by Dawes well saved and the ball almost permanently pinging around the Charlton defence which featured ex-Lion Alan McLeary. It was looking bleak for McCarthy's men when Garry Nelson gave his side the lead just after half time with virtually their only attempt.

Alex Rae came to the rescue again with an equaliser just after the hour mark. Verveer won a free kick and the Scot smashed home from 25 yards to signal another Millwall onslaught as they went in search of the winner.

It was looking as though it wasn't meant to be and a third successive draw would further dent their top two hopes, until Moralee turned inside the crowed Charlton penalty area with Millwall's last attack in injury time. His shot took a deflection off a defender and spun to Rae who was waiting on the edge of the six yard box. With the goalkeeper wrong-footed, he was able to divert the ball into the net to send the crowd berserk.

Three matches against sides struggling at the other end of the table now followed but Millwall seemed to have overcome their Achilles heel with a home win against third-bottom Peterborough but the old demons were back again at Watford when the second-from-bottom Hornets consigned The Lions to just their third league defeat in 21 games - all coming against teams in the bottom third of the table.

Two more points were squandered next - this time at home to 19th-placed Luton where the visitors twice came back to draw 2-2 and it was looking worse at Portsmouth when, with the sides locked at 1-1 going into the final five minutes and Millwall pressing for a winner, Pompey were awarded a spot kick which was duly converted to seemingly send Millwall spinning to another defeat.

Thankfully Mitchell was on hand to salvage a late, late equaliser but The Lions' form had really hit the buffers at the worst possible time once again with just two wins in their last eight games. Thankfully the teams around them were also feeling the pressure with Charlton completely going to pieces losing five on the spin and Derby only managing one win in seven leaving Millwall clinging on to fifth place going into the next home match with Sunderland. Transfer deadline day had seen another experienced player arrive at The Den when Clive Allen was signed to bolster an attack that now boasted Dave Mitchell, John Kerr and a fit-again Jamie Moralee but was missing Goodman who had been injured since the victory over Bolton and wasn't expected to feature again that season. It was a huge blow, Goodman's pace, holding play and ruthlessness in front of goal was invaluable and he was starting to develop a brilliant partnership with Mitchell.

Thankfully Mitchell was still there and scored both goals to help defeat Sunderland 2-1 and send Millwall to table-topping Palace in third place.

Now was the time to grind out a goalless draw. Palace had now stretched their lead at the top having lost just twice in the 17 games since that New Year's Day mauling at Millwall but had played two or three games more than other teams. Overhauling them was still a tall order but second place was very much in Millwall's sights. Forest had hit a little bump with just one win in their last four and were only four points ahead of The Lions having played a game more. Crucially, they had to come to The Den next. Avoiding defeat at Selhurst Park, then beating Forest would put Millwall very much in the driving seat with just six games to go.

Just over an hour had ticked by in a contest that was as tight as a submarine door between a Crystal Palace side looking for those last few points to rubber-stamp their immediate return to the Premier League and a Millwall team knowing that a single point was, for once, a valuable one.

You would almost have imagined that the sides had come to an unspoken agreement that the final third of the match would be played out without incident, giving them both the priceless point they required. Not that the game wasn't being played in a competitive manner of course. The very nature of a local derby, the historic rivalry, the large crowd, meant that both teams were still keen to secure bragging rights if the chance presented itself, but happy not to gamble too much on ending up with nothing.

Then came that sickening finger of cruel fate when Chris Armstrong, the gifted young strike who, 18 months earlier looked to be Millwall's key to a serious promotion challenge, scored the only goal of the game to send Palace ten points clear at the top and Millwall home pointless.

Nottingham Forest had beaten Charlton and so the two teams faced each other in a Sunday afternoon showdown with a fateful message from manager Mick McCarthy in the programme:

"This is one we must win. There's no getting away from the importance of this afternoon's game to us. If we beat Forest then we have every chance of claiming that second automatic promotion spot. If we don't then realistically we're looking for a play-off place."

You could understand the sentiment. Millwall now trailed Forest by seven points and with just 18 to play for after this match, even with a game extra, The Lions would be hard pushed to close that gap. However, it will have heaped even more pressure on an already creaking Lions team.

Endsleigh League Division One - April 14th 1994							
	P	W	D	L	F	A	PTS
1. Crystal Palace	42	24	9	9	68	42	81
2. Nottingham Forest	40	20	11	9	63	42	71
3. Leicester	40	18	11	11	65	53	65
4. Notts County	41	20	5	16	60	61	65
5. MILLWALL	**39**	**17**	**13**	**9**	**51**	**43**	**64**
6. Derby County	40	18	9	13	64	49	63

Another raucous New Den crowd greeted Jamie Moralee's seventh-minute opener like a promotion-clincher and the feeling of relief was palpable from the stands to the pitch but, despite dominating the rest of the first half, Millwall were unable to add to their lead and, early in the second half that man Collymore returned to haunt them once again by grabbing the leveller. It was a bitterly disappointing goal to concede, and not just because Collymore and the Millwall fans were enjoying something of a personal rivalry which stretched back to his days at Southend.

A Forest corner was won in the air by ex-Lion Colin Cooper despite the attentions of two Millwall players and as the ball fell to Collymore on the edge of the six yard box with his back to goal, he was somehow able to turn and score despite being surrounded by three Lions defenders.

After surviving several scares as Forest pushed for a second, Mitchell grabbed the initiative back again seven minutes later when he brilliantly headed home a Cunningham cross from the right hand side and it looked to be enough as the game moved into the final ten minutes.

Millwall had managed to do what they thought would guarantee the points in the event of not adding to their lead: keep Collymore quiet. But it was another lightning quick break from the former Southend and Palace man that led to the equaliser. His scuffed shot appeared to be rolling safely across the Millwall goal but wasn't picked up by a home defender, leaving Ian Woan to collect it from the left touchline and recycle it via the on-rushing Stuart Pearce. Fearing the veteran defender's venomous left foot, Millwall swarmed around him and, deterred from letting fly, he played it back out to Woan.

The Millwall rearguard was now playing catch-up having expected a Pearce blockbuster, allowing Forest defender Steve Stone to run into the space vacated at Millwall's near post and met Woan's inch-perfect cross with a deft header into the top corner of Kasey Keller's net.

That killer goal had come at the home end - which was at the time still known as its rather sterile 'South Stand' moniker in the days before it took on the more familiar Cold Blow Lane name. As at the old Den, Millwall had always favoured attacking the home/Cold Blow Lane end in the second half and, more often than not, were able to do so. When Brian Clough's Forest visited The Den in a First Division encounter back in 1988, Clough, always with an attention to detail in order to gain even the slightest psychological advantage, forced Millwall to attack the home end in the first half which made for unfamiliar viewing for home fans. That day it was enough to put them off their stride for 80 minutes as Forest took a 2-0 lead, but Millwall fought back to draw 2-2. Now, with the same subtle disturbance in The Den's equilibrium, Forest had this time been the ones to snatch a late draw. This of course is the problem with statements such as McCarthy's in that day's programme. The opportunity to beat Forest was there, it had gone, and suddenly, with just one fateful attack, Millwall were looking at the play-offs instead of automatic promotion.

To compound their misery, the defeat to Palace and draw with Forest had pushed them down to seventh place, ringing frightening alarm bells of last season's late capitulation. Such was the congestion in that top six however that a single goal victory at home to Wolves courtesy of another Mitchell goal three days later was enough to send Millwall back up to third and provide a huge psychological boost.

Tranmere had recovered from their mid-season wobble to make a return appearance in the play-off zone and Millwall once again chose the worst possible time to put in one of their poorest displays of the season. Veteran striker John Aldridge's second goal of the game in the first minute of the second half gave Millwall a 3-0 mountain to climb and despite a late rally with goals from Moralee and Kerr it was a second defeat in four to leave Lions fans nervously looking over their shoulders again.

Yet again Millwall failed to see off relegation-haunted opposition when Luton were allowed to take their second point of the season off The Lions and as Millwall prepared for the final home league match of the season against Bristol City everything was up in the air.

Millwall sat in fifth place on 69 points with three games left but just five points separated them from tenth placed Middlesbrough. As in the previous season, Leicester and Tranmere's late runs had seen them all but secure a play-off berth, while Palace and Forest could relax having secured automatic promotion.

With tricky final matches away to Barnsley and Grimsby - two venues that Millwall had rarely enjoyed fruitful visits to - three points against Bristol City was imperative.

It was to be more frustration for The Lions though who failed to break down one of the few teams in the division that had absolutely nothing left to play for and the goalless draw dropped them below Derby into sixth place.

Thankfully though, luck was on Millwall's side for once. Notts County's 3-3 draw with Charlton ended their hopes of grabbing sixth place as did Wolves' defeat to Barnsley. Stoke's draw with Leicester put paid to their hopes meaning Millwall were virtually guaranteed a play-off place, with a game to spare.

That easing of the pressure was evident as they defeated Barnsley 1-0 at Oakwell thanks to another late Mitchell goal and even a solitary point in a goalless draw at Grimsby was enough to propel them into play-off pole position of third on a bizarre day that saw both Tranmere and Derby lose and Leicester draw.

Derby would be Millwall's opponents in The Lions' second ever play-off adventure and, as with the two-legged affair against Brighton four years earlier, Millwall would hold the supposed advantage of playing the second leg in front of their home fans. The big question was this time, could they avoid disaster in the first match to give themselves a chance?

15

It's The Hope That Kills You

◇◇◇◇◇◇◇◇◇◇◇◇◇◇◇◇◇◇◇◇◇◇◇◇◇◇◇◇◇◇

When the idea of the play-offs was announced back in 1986, I can guarantee you that Millwall fans the world over of a certain age will have been thinking one thing: "Only a matter of time before we come a cropper with them".

Not only were the play-offs just what the game needed, they were a perfect setting for more Millwall fan misery. So it proved in 1990 when, The Lions looked odds on to, at the very least, earn themselves a first trip to Wembley since 1945 for a chance to bounce straight back to the top flight.

Despite the Millwall way of expecting the worst and the glass being half full, even the most cynical would have gone into that inaugural play-off campaign with confidence.

Everything was on their side then. They faced

an opponent they had taken four points off in league matches, and had home advantage for the crucial second leg of the semi-final. They even took a first half lead in the initial game. What could possibly go wrong?

As with most football fans, nuanced is not a term that applies to many scenarios - and especially so at Millwall.

Football, by its very competitive sporting nature is black and white. There are winners, and losers. There is success and failure. In the eyes of fans, life is either fantastic, or shit. Similarly, players are either great, or useless.

In the space of four seasons, the attitude of Millwall supporters towards their play-off chances had flipped. Outwardly they would still have been confident that a two-legged semi-final with Derby - with whom they had shared two goalless league draws that season - *should* have been winnable. Especially with, once again, the second leg at The Den.

But that confidence was a thin veneer, weakened by the bitter experience of Brighton four years before. The play-offs does this to you. It is truly a peculiar beast. At the start of the season, you, like many of the fans of about two thirds of each division, will have a similar level of expectation:

'We're OK. Not great, but not crap. We won't

get relegated. I don't think we'll be down near the bottom either. If we're not near the bottom, there's a chance we could make the play-offs. We're not good enough for automatic promotion, but the play-offs are definitely a possibility, and if we can get into the play-offs...'

So you talk yourself into this hope and expectation that the play-offs provide and you'll revisit this at various times in the season.

If you lose a few and slip into the bottom half you will scoff at the mere suggestion you could ever make the top six. Yet win three or four in a row after Christmas, and suddenly it's all back on again. The play-offs have a lot to answer for in keeping that hopeful voice in the football fans' head chattering away for that little bit longer and, as we all know, it's the hope that kills you.

Forget what anyone tells you about form going into the play-offs. Most of the time the teams that take part in this end-of-season episode of Russian Roulette are unrecognisable from those that slogged through forty-odd games.

Equally, forget the so-called 'advantage' of finishing higher in the table. I won't bore you with a list of statistics, but the lucky buggers that sneaked a final day sixth place by the skin of their teeth more often than not go on to win the final over teams that had done the double over them during the season and spent most of it knocking on the door of the automatic places.

OK I suppose you couldn't really have a piece like this without a *couple* of stats so here goes:

Unsurprisingly to Millwall supporters, as of 2020, the record for the lowest amount of points earned by a team that went on to win promotion to the top flight via the play-offs is held by Crystal Palace. Well, OK, it was, for 13 years. Palace finished in sixth place in the 1996-97 season with a paltry 71 points, yet brushed aside third-placed Wolves in their semi-final and Sheffield United in the final. The Blades had finished just a place and two points ahead of Palace. Even Wolves' final total of 76 wasn't great, but spare a thought for Sunderland on the flipside who amassed 90 points in the following season (usually enough to win you the title) but failed to win their play-off final. Blackpool took that Palace record off them in 2009-2010 when they finished sixth with 70 points and won promotion to the Premier League.

So if Millwall fans went into the Brighton play-off campaign with a rousing "Come on, let's get at them" battle cry, the approach to facing Derby this season was more "Oh go on then, if we really must, but we know how it's going to end..."

Derby's form going into the play-offs had been dreadful. A single win and two draws from their final five matches, including conceding four in the first half of the final match of the regular campaign away to Southend.

The problem was, as in 1990, Millwall's form wasn't much better than their opponents with just an extra draw from their last five matches. There was hope however that The Lions defence had been far more miserly with just one goal conceded in the final four matches. The single defeat had come in that disappointing first half submission at Tranmere who were facing Leicester in the other semi-final. Having that defeat at Prenton Park fresh in the memory surely wouldn't have helped had The Lions been facing John Aldridge's men again and a trip to Leicester - where they had been thrashed 4-0 earlier in the season also posed the threat of rendering the second leg a dead rubber.

All this speculation of course meant nothing, this was the play-offs, all bets were off, the slate wiped clean, form book out of the window.

Derby were an entirely different proposition to the side that Millwall faced in two goalless games that season and a million miles away from the shambolic defensive mess that had shipped four at Southend a matter of days before. Organised at the back, rapid and menacing going forward, it was no surprise when they took the lead through veteran striker Gordon Cowans midway through the first half.

An aimless clearance from Millwall was casually collected midway in his own half by Forsyth and he sent a long ball back into The Lions half where Johnson headed on to the advancing Gabbiadini.

Gabbiadini's neat overhead kick took him away from Van Den Hauwe who was playing as part of a three central defender system. He cut the ball back from the byline where Simpson was waiting to pounce and round off a stunning move worthy of winning any play-off tie.

Instead, Millwall defender Neil Emblen's desperate attempt to cut out the cross seemed to have done enough to distract Simpson whose mis-hit shot took a deflection off Emblen, bobbled into the post and then back into the grateful arms of Lions' 'keeper Kasey Keller.

Unfortunately it also dropped in the exact position that Simpson's legs had landed after he's stumbled into the six yard box following his goal attempt. Keller was unable to cleanly collect and despite a couple of frantic efforts to scoop the ball up, Simpson was able to flick it away from his out-stretched palms.

The wily Cowans, who had seen this type of scenario played out hundreds of times was lurking, gambling on such an error, and snapped up the opportunity lashing the ball into the net despite more desperate attempts from three Millwall defenders in the six yard box to block.

This felt harsh, but oh so familiar. Derby were constantly getting the better of Millwall's somewhat unfamiliar defensive system and tempers boiled over early in the second half when Gabbiadini was away again but Van Den Hauwe managed to slide in to win the ball after the Derby striker had shown a bit too much of it to the former Everton man.

Somewhat foolishly, Gabbiadini scythed Van Den Hauwe down and chaos ensued. It wasn't clear if the eight or nine players in the ruck that followed were fighting with each other or simply trying to save Gabbiadini from a furious Van Den Hauwe. Either way, Millwall were being rattled and Derby sensed opportunity. Moments later a long free kick was pumped towards the Millwall area from just inside the Derby half by Short. Emblen managed to win the header on the edge of the area but it looped and dropped just a few yards away where Pembridge then enjoyed an outrageous stroke of luck when the ball hit him on the back of the head as Hurlock closed in to lash the ball clear.

Gabbiadini was there again to collect the lose ball and dink it over the Lions back line that were rushing out, by-passing the onside Johnson who had time and space to compose himself and slam the ball into the roof of the net for number two.

It was a cruel rehash of Brighton's equaliser in 1990. That day an unfortunate rebound off the back of Millwall defender Dave Thompson inadvertently played in Barham for Brighton's equaliser and set them up for the win.

This time, the lucky bounce had gone against Millwall yet again.

The match finished 2-0 to Derby. Not quite the disaster of The Goldstone Ground four years before but enough of a mountain to climb for McCarthy's men at The Den three days later.

That mountain became unconquerable after just sixteen minutes of the second leg when Gabbiadini once again proved to be Millwall's tormentor.

It all came from a hopeful attack in a bright start by The Lions. Hurlock did well to keep the ball in on the left and played the ball to Stevens who crossed early to the edge of the Derby area.

His cross was easily dealt with by Harkes and his headed clearance found Pembridge in acres of space in the middle of the pitch.

He was able to run virtually unchallenged into the Millwall half before playing the lightning-quick Johnson in behind the ferociously backpedaling Lions' back line.

His cross was met by the grateful Gabbiadini to slide in and give Derby a 1-0 lead on the night and virtually end the tie at 3-0 on aggregate. Six minutes later play-off humiliation was once again on the cards as Johnson raced clear again to lash home number two. It was like a repeating nightmare for Millwall's fans, and it was about to get much worse.

A chance for Moralee was collected by Derby 'keeper Taylor but as he got to his feet and prepared to release the ball, a fan appeared, running behind him across his goal. One soon became many and instantly referee Brian Hill ordered the players off and to the sanctuary of the changing rooms as mounted police appeared to prevent a full scale pitch invasion. Here, in the debut season of Millwall's new stadium, was a perfect illustration of one of its downfalls against the old Den. With no perimeter fencing, it was easy for fans to gain access to the pitch in seconds. Millwall chairman Reg Burr was hopeful that the days where the need for high fences and rotating spikes were over - especially with Hillsborough still so fresh in the memory. In just a few mad minutes he had been proven painfully wrong. A season that so many hoped would be a brave new dawn for Millwall Football Club and its fans was unravelling in its final act and in the worst possible way.

When play finally resumed, the comedic nature of Derby's third goal summed up Millwall's night. Johnson and Gabbiadini were again involved, but on this occasion it was Millwall's players who were the architects of their own downfall rather than the fans.

Pat Van Den Hauwe calmly intercepted Johnson's mis-placed pass to Gabbiadini but then somehow contrived to play it the other side of the advancing Keller and into his net to make it 3-0 to Derby at half time and 5-0 on aggregate. Greg Berry's consolation on the hour mark sparked an unlikely Millwall surge for more goals but as Alex Rae was sent sprawling in the area by Williams and referee Hill pointed to the spot to award Millwall a penalty, the pitch was once again flooded with fans and brought to a halt.

After a further delay which saw the players back in the dressing rooms for almost fifteen minutes, an incredulous home crowd watched in disbelief as Hill restarted the match with a drop ball to Derby in the centre circle.

The match official later explained that the penalty incident had occurred after fans were on the pitch and he had decided the game should be stopped at this point rather than being allowed to continue to the its spot-kick conclusion.

Not that it mattered of course. A 5-2 defeat is no more use than 5-1, just as the 6-2 defeat to Brighton four years before was no more damaging than any other deficit. At least on that occasion Millwall were just left with the mess of a missed trip to Wembley and another season in the second tier to contemplate.

Now their troubles had only just begun.

Endsleigh League Division One 1993-94 Final Table

Crystal Palace	**46**	**27**	**9**	**10**	**73**	**46**	**+27**	**90**	**Champions**
Nottingham F	**46**	**23**	**14**	**9**	**74**	**49**	**+25**	**83**	**Promoted**
Millwall	46	19	17	10	58	49	+9	74	
Leicester City	**46**	**19**	**16**	**11**	**72**	**59**	**+13**	**73**	**Play-off winners**
Tranmere Rovers	46	21	9	16	69	53	+16	72	
Derby County	46	20	11	15	73	68	+5	71	
Notts County	46	20	8	18	65	69	−4	68	
Wolves	46	17	17	12	60	47	+13	68	
Middlesbrough	46	18	13	15	66	54	+12	67	
Stoke City	46	18	13	15	57	59	−2	67	
Charlton Athletic	46	19	8	19	61	58	+3	65	
Sunderland	46	19	8	19	54	57	−3	65	
Bristol City	46	16	16	14	47	50	−3	64	
Bolton	46	15	14	17	63	64	−1	59	
Southend	46	17	8	21	63	67	−4	59	
Grimsby Town	46	13	20	13	52	47	+5	59	
Portsmouth	46	15	13	18	52	58	−6	58	
Barnsley	46	16	7	23	55	67	−12	55	
Watford	46	15	9	22	66	80	−14	54	
Luton Town	46	14	11	21	56	60	−4	53	
WBA	46	13	12	21	60	69	−9	51	
Birmingham	**46**	**13**	**12**	**21**	**52**	**69**	**−17**	**51**	**Relegated**
Oxford	**46**	**13**	**10**	**23**	**54**	**75**	**−21**	**49**	**Relegated**
Peterborough	**46**	**8**	**13**	**25**	**48**	**76**	**−28**	**37**	**Relegated**

94/95

andy may's dad

16

The Calm After The Storm

The aftermath of the Derby play-off trouble was as expected, on an apocalyptic scale as details began to filter out about the night's events. During the second pitch invasion Derby players were kicked to the ground and a mob of over 1000 ran rampage in the club car park afterwards. Vehicles were damaged, including a BBC Radio Derby car, bricks were hurled at police and six officers required treatment for injuries.

Seventeen people were arrested and eight charged with a variety of offences including criminal damage and breach of the peace.

Millwall were charged by the FA and stadium closure along with heavy fine and points deduction looked a very real possibility.

Even the chairman and manager didn't escape criticism. After the away leg, Burr accused Derby of 'kicking us off the park'. His comments were condemned for inflaming the situation and possibly inciting a desire for revenge among spectators. The finger was also pointed at McCarthy, who was accused, by implication, of calling on the club's followers to make it an intimidating evening for the visiting team. In his programme notes, McCarthy wrote:

'The Derby fans managed to make it a hostile environment for us up there and I know from experience that they cannot hold a candle to the Millwall crowd in this department.'

The familiar dog pile then ensued with other First Division managers pointing to the fact that Millwall had lost only one league game at home all season, suggesting some sort of unfair advantage in the intimidation that greeted away teams at The New Den.

It was a quite ridiculous assertion to make and would normally have been dismissed without the merest consideration. Football has always been about making your home your fortress and nobody ever complained that Liverpool, Leeds or Manchester United had an *unfair* advantage by having a loud, intimidating atmosphere which often lent itself to impressive home form - and therefore success. Of course it was an advantage, but a purely fair and footballing one.

The implication now was of course that teams

would be scared to go to The Den and be unable to perform under normal circumstances. What they were of course looking for was for Millwall to have a *disadvantage* at home during at least the 94/95 season.

The irony was of course that, back in August 1993 after that 4-1 drubbing at the hands of Southend in their new stadium's first ever league match, Millwall fans wondered if they had lost any home advantage the old Den had afforded them. They felt like Samson with his freshly shorn barnet sapping all his strength and power.

Yet they turned it around and enjoyed their best home season since 1984-85. Now it seemed their locks would be trimmed again.

Derby vice-chairman Lionel Pickering, said Millwall should be closed down for good unless the problem was eradicated:

"If you don't put a fence around the ground or dig a moat. . .then I don't see a future for them. You have to stop fans getting on to the pitch and if trouble continues other clubs will refuse to play them."

It was understandable that Derby would be disappointed that for them, a great play-off result was completely overshadowed by the trouble - and to compound that, defeat in the final itself - but it was still a very over-the-top and typically hysterical response. Millwall had learned in the hardest possible way of the shortcomings of their new stadium. To move from what had become an almost stalag like old Den to this plush new arena that offered smooth, freshly concreted walkways almost straight on to the pitch had been a jump too far in the trust of fans when times had become testing. It would be fair to say that almost every other club in the league would have been in favour of that moat, and many would have liked it to be filled with crocodiles to boot.

Reg Burr offered to resign if 'I thought that would make any difference'. He added:

"Naturally we are very upset by what happened. We had over 300 stewards, 200 to 400 police, a number of police horses and deliberately kept the lower north tier empty so there could be no possibility of conflict between the fans. We believe we took every possible precaution."

Millwall were given two weeks to respond, during this time the usual media post mortem took place including a debate on ITV's Sport in Question show.

Chaired by Ian St John and with contributions from Jimmy Greaves and racing expert John McCrirrick, it became nothing more than a kangaroo court played out for the cameras with both Greaves and McCrirrick shouting "send 'em down" like mad judges concluding a murder trial at various stages of the debate.

Fearing the worst, Millwall supporters geared themselves up for a familiar season of decline as is par for the course after such events. Publicly, football managers and players will insist that they are unaffected by incidents like this one. They will try to reinforce the idea that they are shut away in a footballing cocoon and are only bothered about playing football.

The reality must surely be that, when a club suffers an incident on this kind of scale, the fallout must not only shroud the club in a cloud of gloom, but also place winning games of football in a very unsatisfactory back seat. The knock-on effect must therefore be that some managers and players will feel it is holding their careers back as further trouble and sanctions may undo any good work they have achieved on the pitch.

The punishment when it came was surprisingly lenient. There was indeed ground closures and behind closed doors sanctions, but with a suspension of six months. Millwall had been given a massive second chance.

Success often led to incidents of crowd trouble over the years at Millwall, the two seemed to go hand in hand. Now, after two seasons of desperately striving and stretching for success and just missing out, rather than regroup and look to go again, it felt like all Millwall Football Club wanted was a quiet season of mid-table anonymity. Not that they would admit that of course, but the way they club was at that moment in time, as the dust was finally settling on a brutal 1993-94, they just wanted to heal.

They needed a calm after the storm.

A summer tour of Ireland was followed up by two more impressive home friendlies. Portugal provided the opposition once again, as they had done for the stadium's opener twelve months earlier and once again the visiting manager was Bobby Robson who had moved from Sporting Lisbon to Porto during the previous season. Millwall gave a good account of themselves in a 0-1 defeat to his impressive Primeira Divisão side - who would go on to win the title. Porto's squad included Russian internationals Sergei Yuran and Vasili Kulkov, two names to conjure with a bit later in this tale. This was followed up by a 1-1 draw against John Toshack's Spanish top flight side Real Sociedad

The Porto match also saw a debut for another of Millwall's exciting young players with Jermaine Wright featuring in the team, but this was tempered by the fact two other key young squad members had left the club.

Striker Jamie Moralee had signed for Watford for £500,000 and central defender Neil Emblen departed for Wolves for £1million. Moralee had struggled with injuries but, when fully fit, brought pace and, more importantly, goals to the team. Emblen's move was the biggest shock, coming after playing just 12 matches for The Lions.

Signed from non-league Sittingbourne, Emblen immediately impressed but suffered an injury during the New Year's day massacre of Palace. He returned to feature in four of the last six games, making his final appearance in that disastrously reshaped defence that McCarthy sent out in the first leg of the play-off semi-final at Derby.

The big issue for Millwall was that players - and their agents - were just starting to take control of the game over clubs. Agents had long been a necessary evil in football but now the power shift was becoming seismic with the historic Bosman ruling just around the corner. Player agents weren't just negotiating the best deals for the client during transfer negotiations, they were constantly on the lookout for the next big move and payday, in the ear of the player about progressing and reaching the promised land of the Premier League.

What was most annoying for Millwall fans as the latest bright young members of their team headed for The Den's still-shiny new exit doors, was that they had moved to clubs in the same division as Millwall and who had fared worse than The Lions in the previous season. Wolves had not managed a play-off place and Watford had spent most of the season struggling to avoid the drop to the third tier.

Supporters simply couldn't get their head around the mentality of a player leaving a club that had finished third for one finishing seventh - and certainly not seventeenth!

The harsh reality was probably that, the players' respective agents would have found the task of persuading them to move a relatively easy one given the negative publicity that had descended like a huge dark cloud over the club.

Another less surprising but more poignant departure was that of Terry Hurlock. His short-term deal had expired at the season's end and the return for the Lions legend had not been the sensation that fans would have dreamed of. Suffice to say it was punctuated in typical Hurlock style with his dismissal in the eighth minute of his second home debut for the club. He was snapped up by Fulham who were at that time playing in the league's bottom division. Fortunately many Millwall fans were able to say farewell when he appeared for his new club in a pre-season friendly at Dulwich Hamlet. The move meant that, when he made his Fulham debut, he had played in all four of the English League divisions and Scotland's top flight. He made 27 appearances for Fulham, scoring one goal and amassing a record 61 disciplinary points as his side narrowly missed out on a place in the play-offs. His career was ended by a double fracture of the leg sustained in a pre-season friendly the following summer against his first league club Brentford and he was forced to retire at the age of 36.

The football league fixture computer appeared to have a rather dark sense of humour when it spat out the opening fixtures for the 1994-95 campaign. First visitors to The New Den would be, once again, Southend. The only team who had so far managed to beat Millwall in a league match at the new stadium. Quite how long fans would have to endure it being called 'The New Den' for wasn't yet clear, at least 'The New London Stadium' had been dropped. As it seemed had Ogden Entertainments whose prowess in the event world struggled to extend to Bermondsey save the odd boxing bout.

Next up would be Derby. That's right, Millwall would face the only two teams to beat them at their stadium the previous season in their first two league matches of the new season. Obviously of far more significance for that Derby visit would be the non-footballing nature of their previous meeting.

If Millwall wanted a quiet, sedate start to the new season they had no chance, but at least they still had their sponsor. Captain Morgan were understandably unimpressed by their brand being advertised on the front pages of the nationals press and television news in between police horses attempting to clear fans from the pitch, but they had agreed to honour the three year deal that had initially been agreed.

It had been a real slap in the face for director Peter Mead though.

Mead had worked tirelessly since the First Division days to secure a lucrative big-name sponsor. One like Captain Morgan that would have helped investment to improve the club's chances of remaining in the top flight.

At the time he was rebuffed by every major brand he approached (and as a director of one of the world's leading advertising agencies, he approached a lot).

The reasons they gave almost always boiled down to the same thing: Panorama. The programme that had been the first to tag and label football hooliganism and in the same fell swoop, demonise Millwall - the club it decided to focus on.

That was aired in 1977, Mead was still having it rammed down his throat in 1989. Now just twelve months after finally securing such a deal in 1993, the very worst had happened. He must have had a thousand 'told you sos' ringing around his head.

The season opened up into a frustrating symmetry to the previous one. Southend were comfortably beaten in the opener and Derby were hammered 4-1 thanks to a John Kerr hat-trick. How Millwall could have done with that result just a few months earlier. It meant an encouraging opening league position of second, but it was still only August.

Then, in complete contrast to the previous season's impressive unbeaten run after a dodgy start, Millwall failed to register a victory in their next ten league matches. The only bright spot being a thrilling comeback at Molineux where Wolves went into a 3-1 lead in the 80th minute only for goals from Cadette and Goodman in the last four minutes to earn a draw for The Lions. Richard Cadette had been signed initially on loan from Falkirk and would soon make the move permanent. The move was a mystery initially to Millwall fans who had been impressed with the strike force of Mitchell and Goodman and the continued progress of Mark Kennedy suggested the team's attack at least was in good hands. Goodman in particular was in fine form with nine goals to his name already so they weren't sure why they needed another striker in an already large squad.

They'd find out soon enough.

By the end of October Millwall were languishing in 22nd place so victory at home to Sheffield United was a welcome relief. Goodman was on target again and Cadette grabbed his third in three with the last-minute winner against his former club. It wasn't enough to keep them out of the bottom three though:

Endsleigh League Division One - October 30th 1994

	P	W	D	L	F	A	PTS
19. Sheffield Utd	14	4	4	6	15	14	16
20. Port Vale	14	4	4	6	15	20	16
21. Bristol City	14	4	4	6	11	13	16
22. MILLWALL	**14**	**3**	**6**	**5**	**19**	**21**	**15**
23. WBA	14	3	4	7	12	22	13
24. Notts County	14	1	5	8	15	25	8

A pleasant distraction was a rare League Cup run. A two-legged victory over Sunderland saw them into a third round visit to Mansfield where victory set up a fourth round tie at Nottingham Forest. Two first half goals from Greg Berry stunned their Premier League opponents and they held out for a 2-0 victory and a place in the last eight of the competition.

Swindon would be Millwall's quarter final opponents in the tie to be played at The County Ground early in the new year and hopes were high after The Lions defeated The Robins 2-1 away at the start of November.

It was a fifth league game unbeaten and Goodman had scored again taking him into double figures. He was showing the attacking quality that Millwall had been lacking for the previous two seasons and had matured into a great leader of the line.

The climb back up the table had begun and, although still down in 19th place, were just two wins away from the fringes of the play-off pack. McCarthy had also moved to strengthen his defence with the signing of centre-back Tony Witter who went straight into the side and immediately impressed.

Suddenly Millwall looked to have quality right through the team with a good blend of youth and experience. Youth products Ben Thatcher and Andy Roberts were now regulars and while there were still a few kinks to be ironed out, the future looked unexpectedly bright.

Then the clouds gathered once more.

Grimsby defeated The Lions with the only goal of the game but it wasn't the scoreline that disappointed the hardy souls that travelled to Blundell Park to cheer on their team. They had felt defeated before the match had even started when it was announced that both Kenny Cunningham and Jon Goodman had been sold to Wimbledon.

17

Drinking in the Last Chance Saloon

If the swiftness of Goodman and Cunningham's departure was hard enough to take, the paltry fee that Millwall received from Wimbledon for two of the most talented young players the club had discovered was devastating.

The reported combined fee of £1.3million was ludicrously low in the climate of ever-increasing transfer fees now that Sky had started to splash the cash with their Premier League television deal. It smacked, once again, of desperation and of Millwall snapping the hand off at the first genuine offer received.

Fans were given the same old routine: 'finances dictated', 'the club has to balance the books', all stock phrases that supporters were sick of hearing. In their eyes, once again, just as Millwall had found what looked like a formula for success, it was sold from under them to a local rival. What made it all the harder to swallow was that this time, instead of being Crystal Palace, it was their Selhurst Park tenants Wimbledon. A club that didn't even have their own stadium were now treating Millwall like a feeder club to help strengthen their place in the top flight while The Lions sold off the family silver to fund their Premier League standard ground.

The programme for the Barnsley home match prompted just a single line explanation from Mick McCarthy about their departure suggesting he was just as perplexed as the fans about the move.

In an unprecedented move, there was even a piece from one of the departed players themselves as Kenny Cunningham explained how much of a wrench it was for him to leave the club and of his sympathy for McCarthy whose hand was clearly forced.

There were far more wide-reaching implications for these moves than mere weakening of the team however. Furious fans planned a demonstration at the Barnsley match, news which had Reg Burr on high alert and he acted quickly to try and block any threat of the merest disturbance at The Den with that suspended sentence still hanging over the club. Promising a face to face meeting with fans at The Den later in the month, Burr made his appeal via the South London Press:

"I am pleading with people not to do anything stupid that could do irreparable damage to the club. There are many people in and out of the game just waiting for us to step out of line again so they can do us more harm. After what happened against Derby we are drinking at the last chance saloon. Many of these people thought we got off lightly during the summer, but any sort of pitch invasion or demonstration and they'll be down on us like a ton of bricks. I do understand people's anger and frustration and why they want to have a go at me. That's why I am proposing a public meeting, at the club, to give the fans a chance to say what they want directly at me".

Burr had a unique way of addressing fans not as a chairman but more as a grudgingly respected teacher or parent. Not because his messages were patronising in tone, but because of their refreshing lack of bullshit and business speak which most used.

The subtext of the average chairman's address to supporters (if he could actually be bothered) was "I'm a businessman, this is business, I wouldn't expect you plebs to understand..." But not Burr. He spoke almost as a fan, it was just unfortunate that on most occasions his message was one that fans perhaps did not want to hear but could not argue with. He was of course spot on. The football authorities wouldn't care if a pitch invasion at the Barnsley match was out of protest for the club selling two of its players. The media certainly wouldn't and, as Burr suggested, would have a field day with it.

The neutral or opposition onlooker also wouldn't accept any mitigating circumstances and the merest of misdemeanours would have cries for the club to be buried from all quarters.

Mercifully the feared trouble didn't materialise. In fact the players were inconspicuous by their absence too as Millwall crumbled to a tame 1-0 defeat to their Yorkshire rivals.

When Mark Burke scored Port Vale's injury time winner in the 2-1 defeat at Vale Park the following week, Lions fans were fearing the worst. Three league defeats in a row since the departure of Goodman and Cunningham saw them back on the edge of the relegation places and with morale seemingly at an all time low both on and off the pitch, it was hardly the best preparation for a trip to Premier League Nottingham Forest in the League Cup. That totally unexpected 2-0 victory at Forest sparked a remarkable recovery however and a galvanised Millwall, with Mitchell and Cadette rediscovering their scoring boots, a remarkable unbeaten run up to Christmas, which featured six consecutive wins (five without conceding including the cup win) and saw them fly up the table to thirteenth. The new year started with draws against Charlton and Oldham as preparation for two huge cup matches in four days. One of which would have Reg Burr squirming uncomfortably in his seat once more.

Millwall had again drawn Arsenal - the third time in successive seasons and the second home FA Cup draw in a row - but the spotlight was on this one more than ever before, even though the suspended sentence period for their FA punishment had now been successfully negotiated. That didn't matter, any more trouble and the retribution would surely be immediate.

Thankfully there was again nothing to report on or off the pitch in a rather dull 0-0 draw which posed more than just the problem of a fixture congestion: A trip to Highbury and the threat of more trouble.

Before that Millwall travelled to Swindon hopeful of reaching the League Cup semi finals for the first time in their history. Having already won at Swindon in the league, hopes were high that they could win through to a last four that would include Crystal Palace and Liverpool, especially given The Lions upturn in form, nine match unbeaten run and the fact that Swindon were without a win in their last fourteen. Those stats of course mean nothing in a one-off cup tie and so it was to prove as Millwall's dreams of a last four two-legged chance to reach the final were obliterated in ten first half minutes when goals from Mutch and Fjortoft put the tie out of The Lions' reach. A late Mitchell consolation was all they had to show in a bitterly disappointing 3-1 defeat.

League form was still impressive though with young defender Mark Beard scoring his first goal for the club in a creditable 1-1 draw away to fifth-placed Sheffield United.

Beard's second goal came in the next match, but in far more dramatic circumstances.

Arriving at Highbury for their FA Cup replay, Millwall showed they had nothing to lose against a nervous Gunners side with an increasingly under fire George Graham clinging on to his job.

The Lions looked confident from the first whistle and there was little surprise when Beard lashed home the opener after just ten minutes in front of a shocked North Bank. McCarthy's men eased through the remainder of the half and rarely looked threatened in the second period, almost adding to their score on several occasions.

As the match ticked into its final moments and the nerves started to jangle amongst the thousands of travelling Millwall fans on the packed Clock End, Mark Kennedy picked up a lose ball just inside his own half on the left hand side.

Rather than head for the corner to run down the clock, the young striker strode into the uncharacteristic gaping hole that had appeared in the centre of the Arsenal defence. As he broke into the Gunners' penalty area still unchallenged he let fly with a scorching shot that ripped into the back of Seaman's net sending the Millwall end behind the goal into complete pandemonium.

It was an historic win for McCarthy's men and by no means a fluke. They had dominated the game and been in complete control throughout. Graham would be sacked by Arsenal a month later. Whilst it wasn't directly responsible for the former Millwall manager's downfall who had been implicated in a charge of financial irregularities regarding some Arsenal transfer payments, it certainly made the decision an easier one for the Arsenal board to make.

Millwall's reward for beating Arsenal would be another big London home tie against Chelsea. This would once again be a double-edged sword for the club and another major headache for Burr and his board. It would be yet another high profile match putting Millwall's fans in the spotlight as much as their players with the history of bad blood between the two clubs. A first ever meeting at the new stadium with its far more relaxed perimeter crowd control features compared to the old Den will have no doubt caused Burr some more sleepless nights.

Thankfully, for once, the hooligan spotlight was taken off Millwall and shone in another corner of south London. Crystal Palace was the venue for the latest episode of football thuggery, but it occurred in the most unbelievable way possible.

After being sent off for Manchester United during their 1-1 draw at Selhurst Park, Eric Cantona lept into the home crowd aiming first a karate kick and then punches at a Palace supporter who had verbally abused the Frenchman as he left the pitch.

The fallout was huge and Cantona even spent time at the local South Norwood police station after he and teammate Paul Ince were arrested for their part in the remarkable brawl that ensued. For once Millwall were out of the headlines when it came to the unsavory side of the game, and with Chelsea arriving at The Den three days later, they prayed it would stay that way.

Another uneventful goalless draw was played

out in another trouble-free afternoon at a packed Den and the unbeaten league run was stretched to nine with a 2-0 home win over Grimsby that saw Mark Kennedy score his eighth of the season. The young striker was being utilised in a wide role and looking more impressive with every game - certainly way beyond his 18 years - and the fear was already circulating amongst Millwall fans that he would be the next player sold off.

Kennedy was one of four first team regulars to have progressed from the youth team, a figure not matched since the FA Youth Cup winning side of 1979 provided the first teams of the subsequent seasons with ten.

Admiring glances were also being directed at his young graduate colleagues Andy Roberts and Ben Thatcher. With little hope of Millwall mounting a tilt at the Premier League this season, it was looking increasingly ominous that another player exodus could be on the cards.

After The Lord Mayor's Show

18

End of Dawes

◇◇◇◇◇◇◇◇◇◇◇◇◇◇◇◇◇◇◇◇◇◇◇◇◇◇◇◇◇◇

The Lions travelled to Stamford Bridge to face their third Premier League opposition away from home in cup competitions, and yet again they more than matched their loftier opponents.

Despite having the better opportunities though, they looked to be heading out when Stein scored for Chelsea with less than twenty minutes to go.

Just eight minutes later however an inch-perfect ball from the impressive Tony Witter found Thatcher on the left hand side deep in the Chelsea half. His bobbling cross eluded virtually everyone and was only scuffed clear by a Chelsea defender into the path of the onrushing Dave Savage who had only been introduced to the action fifteen minutes earlier in place of Alistair Edwards. He calmly stroked home the equaliser to send the travelling fans wild. There was a heart-stopping moment for Millwall's officials when celebrating fans spilled out of the stands and on the touchline to celebrate but they were quickly ushered back to the places by a furious McCarthy and the game ended 1-1.

Extra time was unable to separate the teams and the match went to penalties, a conclusion that had never ended well for Millwall with defeat in their last shoot-out at home to Arsenal two seasons before the latest in a line of spot kick failures.

In a typically heart-stopping decider with The Lions taking first, both teams managed to successfully convert each of their first four penalties. Alex Rae stepped up to take Millwall's fifth and duly despatched it past Dmitri Kharine to put the pressure on young John Spencer to take the action into sudden death.

Spencer's nervy spot-kick was placed at a perfect height to Kasey Keller's left and he comfortably parried it away to win the tie for Millwall and send them into the fifth round.

In such circumstances trouble was almost inevitable. Millwall fans remained in the temporary stand where they had been accommodated, behind a deep wall of police officers as Chelsea fans attempted to reach them from the opposite end, only to be somewhat comically corralled by a troupe of mounted bobbies. The BBC coverage was somewhat typical of the slant given by the media when crowd disturbances are initiated by Premier League clubs.

Des Lynam's immediate post match comments led on the 'trouble' and he handed back live to commentator Barry Davies at a now empty Stamford Bridge.

Davies proceeded to describe 'faces of unacceptable aggression' but instantly gave Chelsea the benefit of the doubt when he described the pitch invasion as 'the threat from what I assume were Chelsea supporters from that end...' and then quite bizarrely mentioned a 'stand-off' at one of the pubs outside as fans left the ground.

One can only assume how the description of events would have been changed if the boot had been on the other foot. Needless to say Millwall received little praise for their exploits, but thankfully no sanctions either. This was quickly becoming a season where Millwall Football Club were living on the very edge of their nerves with every passing high profile game. The draw which sent them to another Premier League London club in QPR would, they hoped, once again pass without incident. On the pitch it was a shame that McCarthy's team failed to get the credit it deserved from outside the confines of The Den. He had constantly proved an astute spotter of a player, regularly introducing virtual unknowns and rejects into the team with surprising results. Players that were catching the eye that season were defenders Tony Witter and Jason van Blerk and attacking midfielder Dave Savage.

Witter had been released by QPR and had been a revelation at the heart of Millwall's defence with his pacey play out from the back and van Blerk - a free transfer from Dutch outfit Go Ahead Eagles - was also exciting to watch with his pacey forays down the left hand side proving to be a useful back-up for Ben Thatcher and could also be used in midfield.

Dublin-born Savage had been brought in from League of Ireland side Longford Town and, like many Irish imports at Millwall, had settled well and quickly endeared himself to Lions fans. It was actually his second attempt to make it in English football having been signed by Brighton as a 17-year-old after impressing at Kilkenny City. The move didn't work out however and he returned to Ireland a year later. After a trial at Scottish side Raith Rovers, he did enough to earn himself a contract offer, but Millwall's scouts north of the border were alerted and he was invited to play for The Lions' reserves. McCarthy was at the match and was so impressed by Savage he offered him a contract and, just to make sure Millwall didn't miss out, drove him in his car to The Den to sign it! In a matter of months Savage had gone from playing in front of 300 fans in the League of Ireland to scoring at Stamford Bridge in front of almost ten times that amount.

Such was the fixture congestion caused by both of Millwall's cup runs and replays, their next match was their fifth round tie at Rangers, their sixth cup match in their last eight games. This time the roles were reversed with Millwall frustrating their top flight opponents and the match looked to be heading for another 0-0 draw and another replay. Lions fans would have been savouring the opportunity to take on QPR on their own patch and fancied a chance of reaching the last eight of the FA Cup when Rangers were awarded a penalty after Lions' defender Damien Webber inexplicably handled an innocent-looking Andy Impey cross and Clive Wilson tucked away the resultant spot-kick to effectively end Millwall's season.

Probably the saddest news for Millwall fans at that time - although they obviously didn't know it yet - was that legendary defender Ian Dawes had played his last game for the club. The former QPR full back had been struggling with a knee injury all season but was desperate to play in the replay at Stamford Bridge and then of course again against his former team in the next round.

He was withdrawn after 76 minutes at Chelsea and failed to recover to make what would have been a fitting final Millwall appearance at Loftus Road. He was just one absentee of many as Millwall resumed league action three days later with a trip to Barnsley. Also missing were Stevens, Mitchell, Rae and Kennedy as the unbeaten league run came to a spectacular end with a thumping 4-1 defeat. Rae returned for the 0-0 home draw with promotion-chasing Middlesbrough but with his squad still ravaged by injury, McCarthy once again went on a recruitment drive. Making their debuts that day were two ex Manchester City strikers: David Oldfield and Jason Beckford. Australian Oldfield had enjoyed a good spell at Leicester after leaving City and joined on loan. Beckford was one of football's nomads, having played at Blackburn, Port Vale, Birmingham, Bury and Stoke after leaving his native Manchester and yet was still only 25.

Millwall were back to winning ways and cementing their place right in the middle of the table when they beat Swindon 3-1 at The Den courtesy of two goals from Rae and one from van Blerk. Swindon's season had nose-dived and they were now languishing in the relegation places after starting the season as promotion hopefuls and reaching the last four of the League Cup at The Lions' expense. The fact that Millwall completed an easy league double over them only served to make that quarter final cup defeat all the harder to take. A draw at Luton was followed by a club first when the home match with Reading saw Millwall start with two Australian strikers. Both David Oldfield (born in Perth Australia but moved to England and represented them at under 21 level) and Dave Mitchell (born in Glasgow but moved to Australia and represented them at international level) were on target in a 2-0 win over The Royals. The pair were on target again in the next two matches but could not prevent Millwall slumping to defeat at Derby then Portsmouth - both by the odd goal in five. The losing run was extended to four with a 1-0 home loss to Rioch's promotion-bound Bolton and a shocker at relegation-haunted West Brom where they went down 3-0.

Those two defeats put Millwall in the rare position of being one of a small number of teams going into the final nine matches of the season with little chance of a play-off place and no realistic threat of relegation. Home wins over Tranmere and another away to Burnley saw Millwall coasting towards the season's end, but once again the other of the twin spectres of Millwall's past revisited fans to haunt them again. In a move that almost mirrored the chain of events that saw brilliant youngster Kevin O'Callaghan leave the club some fifteen years earlier, Mark Kennedy was sold to Liverpool for a deal worth up to £2.3million. As with the O'Callaghan move, the deal represented a then British transfer record for a teenager. The move came as the end of March transfer deadline approached but also culminated, almost immediately with that loss at home to Bolton which effectively ended any chances Millwall had of making the play-offs.

Whether extended promotion chances for Millwall would have made any difference is neither here nor there. For many fans this was the final straw. In a season that should, in their eyes, have seen the club add quality to an exciting young squad and go one better than the previous season to clinch automatic promotion to the Premier League, they had instead sold off the family silver and replaced it with rusting old junk. Emblen, Moralee, Cunningham, Goodman and now Kennedy represented five first team starters that brought defensive stability with pacey attacking flair - and goals. No club can afford to give away such assets in such a short space of time and not expect repercussions both in results and morale. Millwall's was now at an all time low, although in typically bullish style, McCarthy was trying to make the best of what must have been, for him, an increasingly frustrating and difficult job to do.

In an attempt to spin this latest devastating departure, chairman Burr explained in an interview given to the South London Press, that McCarthy would get "most of the money from the sale to build a promotion-winning side next season" and that the deal had been agreed during a six-hour board meeting that included McCarthy where it appears the prime motivation behind accepting the Liverpool bid was not, as fans would assume, more financial fire-fighting, but to fund the purchase of two strikers.

As we've already established, as football chairmen go, Reg Burr was one of the better ones. The role of a football club chairman is an invidious one at the best of times - and none more so than being Millwall's. If Burr had a failing, you'd have to say that it was his honesty. Candour filled his latest quotes again:

"We analysed the team and it's clear the reason we have failed to get promotion when we should have done in the past three seasons is a lack of goals," he explained.

"It doesn't matter what League you're playing

in, the First Division or the Lewisham and Bermondsey League, you have got to have 40 odd goals coming from the front two or you won't go up."

"This is a strategic move so Mick can go out and buy the strikers who will hopefully help us launch a challenge next season."

And he moved to assure fans that their other Lions favourites would still be there at the start of the next campaign:

"I cannot conceive of a situation where we would want or need to sell a major player now or in the summer."

That last sentence sounded like the kiss of death for Millwall's long-suffering fans.

There were two very big issues with this statement. One, and the most jaw-droppingly outrageous one for fans reading it, was that it sounded like Millwall were selling a player in order to buy two more - who were needed to do the job that two players Millwall had sold in the previous nine months were more than capable of doing! For Millwall fans, it seemed far more sensible to keep the likes of Moralee and Goodman who had proved they could both score goals at this level which may well have ensured that Millwall would by now be vying for a top two promotion place instead of selling yet another star player - who also weighed in with goals - to finance two more.

Lions fans of a certain age will have been fearful of Millwall's attempts to buy success and its disastrous consequences when then then chairman Alan Thorne provided Peter Anderson with an unprecedented war chest which almost sent them into Division Four in 1983. Burr of course had faith in his own ultimately more successful squad financing project which resulted in promotion to the top flight in 1988. Either way it was a gamble and both the table Millwall were playing at - and the game they were playing - was now a very different one to that of 1987. The stakes were on a completely different level.

Secondly, Burr was making the age-old mistake in football administration that almost always comes back to bite you on the arse: a promise not to sell any players.

Honesty, like a little knowledge, can be a very dangerous thing. However Burr and McCarthy tried to spin it, Lions fans were both angry and disappointed, and it would soon be shown in very bizarre circumstances.

Fortunately Oldfield *was* impressing fans, having grabbed two at Turf Moor and he was joined by another experienced striker who marked his debut with a goal. Kerry Dixon had broken all goalscoring records in his time at Chelsea and now at the age of 34 he was keen to extend his career after short spells at Southampton and Luton. It took him a little over an hour to open his Millwall account in the 2-1 win over Tranmere and Oldfield was on target again with his fifth in eight games in the 3-1 home loss to Port Vale. That loss was described by McCarthy as the worst performance since he took over as manager but entered fan folklore for entirely different reasons. As the visitors coasted to victory and Millwall fans voiced their disgust, a lone supporter suddenly appeared on the pitch. There was little need for alarm however as this particular pitch invader was not the usual marauding young character you'd usually associate with such incidents.

Decidedly middle-aged in appearance, dressed smartly in sports jacket, collared shirt, trousers and shoes and looking a little unsteady on his feet, he staggered towards the centre circle where he promptly sat down in protest. Thankfully the even the vultures of the nation's media saw the funny side of this and whilst pictures appeared in the papers the next day, Millwall didn't need to fear any FA retribution on this occasion.

The most comical aspect of the image was of Lions' midfielder Andy May in the background with a decidedly resigned look on his face and hands planted firmly on hips. Millwall fanzine *The Lion Roars* used the image for the front cover of their next edition and, pointing out the passing resemblance between the rogue fan and Millwall midfield maestro, promptly dubbed him 'Andy May's Dad' which has stuck to this day.

Dixon scored his second for the club in a routine 3-1 win over Charlton at The Den in a match that saw youngster Lee McRobert score his first goal for the club in the second minute. McRobert had been signed from non-league Sittingbourne and given a surprise early introduction to First Division football in McCarthy's injury-hit squad.

Leaving The Den was popular striker Dave Mitchell. 'Beadle' had quickly become a favourite with fans with his no-nonsense play and had scored some crucial and memorable goals for Millwall. With the end of his playing career approaching, he had accepted an offer from top Malaysian side Selangor which enabled him to be closer to his Australian-based family. His departure had unfortunately been leaked before he had chance to announce it officially in the programme for the Charlton match. More blanks were drawn in a 1-0 defeat at Watford and goalless draw at home to Notts County and in a season that Millwall fans were quickly hoping to the see the back of, they were treated to an away win at Oldham courtesy of a Savage goal and a seven goal thriller away to Stoke. Millwall twice clawed their way back into the game thanks to first half equalisers from Dixon and Webber and Oldfield gave them a 3-2 lead five minutes after the break but Gleghorn equalised for The Potters ten minutes later and a last minute Kevin Keen goal sealed the points for the home side in a match which encapsulated Millwall's entire season in 90 minutes.

The season rumbled to an end with another bland dead rubber 1-1 draw with relegated Bristol City.

For Millwall fans it had been one of the strangest seasons in living memory. The drama of two fine cup runs where three Premier League teams had been defeated on their own grounds on the way to the last eight and last sixteen of the League and FA Cups had been tempered by a thoroughly anonymous league campaign that had seen neither a challenge for the promotion places or the merest threat of the drop.

In fact, cup games aside, if you had to press Millwall supporters on what was their most memorable moment of a nondescript season, most would probably have said: "Andy May's Dad".

19

Going Uwe The Top

◇◇◇◇◇◇◇◇◇◇◇◇◇◇◇◇◇◇◇◇◇◇◇◇◇◇◇◇◇

If Millwall's board of directors had been brutally honest, the ditchwater-dull season that was 1994-95 was just what the doctor ordered. It had given them time to regroup and to allow the furore of that night against Derby to finally ebb away.

Thankfully there was plenty more for the hand-wringing harbingers of football's doom to dwell on as Cantona's Crystal Palace Kung Fu caper was still one of the major talking points.

Millwall had disgraced themselves it's true but, like a family member scolded for a pissed-up punch up at a family do, they had proved they could behave themselves and were forgiven. For now.

Real disaster had been averted and that was financial doom and relegation - as had beset them following the Ipswich trouble in 1978. Now they were able to make plans once more. Plans to finally make it to the Premier League. Recent heartbreaks had proved that the play-off route was fatally flawed. If they were going to do it they needed to do it properly: top two, as Champions.

Whilst they had enjoyed various success with a variety of striker permutations during the previous season, what was essential was to have two proven scorers at that level.

The rebuilding process came as a complete shock to most Millwall supporters. Admittedly it wasn't on the scale of 1987, but when McCarthy made his first two signings of the summer, they had to sit up and take notice.

First Chris Malkin was signed from Tranmere. Malkin had been a huge part of the Wirral club's rise from the bottom division to the verge of the Premier League with 60 goals in 200 appearances. More importantly, he was a regular goalscorer in the First Division.

The next signing really came out of the blue. German forward Uwe Fuchs had impressed during his loan spell at Middlesbrough the previous season and, when his nine goals in 13 loan appearances helped win 'Boro the First Division title it was assumed the big physical forward would make his move from Bundesliga Kaiserslauten permanent and go on to make his mark in the Premier League.

The Teesside club decided against offering him a permanent deal however and McCarthy was quick to step in and offer him a contract at The Den.

The fee was never confirmed but rumoured to be close to the club record £800,000 Millwall had paid Derby for Paul Goddard back in 1990. Fans could only pray that this investment would prove more fruitful.

Burr had been true to his word, the Kennedy cash had been used to finance deals for two strikers who had a proven goalscoring record at the level The Lions were playing along with a wealth of youthful home-grown talent and experience in their defence and midfield.

It was this midfield however where the next controversial change was made. In a move that probably also helped to fund the Malkin and Fuchs signings, Millwall's midfield starlet Andy Roberts moved to Selhurst Park to join newly-relegated Crystal Palace. This initially sickening news was sweetened a little by the acquisition of not one but two young Palace midfielders in return: Ricky Newman and Bobby Bowry.

Both Newman and Bowry had been lauded as future stars for both club and country at the outset of their careers and, once the slightly disconcerting news that yet another young Millwall star had been sold to a local rival had sunk in, Millwall fans consoled themselves with the thought that they may have got the better of the deal for once, but there was more.

Mark Beard left for fellow Division One side Sheffield United in another baffling deal - worth in the region of £120,000. The young defender's departure meant that almost an entire young, homegrown, or at least locally-scouted back four had left the club in the last 12 months.

Add that to the departure of Goodman, Moralee and Kennedy and it suddenly felt like Millwall were taking a huge gamble with recruitment, going against the proven club ethos of a young, hungry, and largely home-grown or local side. Despite this slightly uneasy feeling however, Lions fans looked forward to the start of the new season with guarded optimism.

Surely the addition of Malkin, Fuchs, Bowry and Newman could help catapult Millwall from mid-table mediocrity to the very top and the promised land of the Premier League in what would be one of the most open First Divisions in years?

As the new season approached confidence grew. Millwall fans scanning the squads of the opposition couldn't really see much to compare in terms of talent, experience and goalscoring potency.

The nineties were only half way through and yet Millwall fans had already dealt with the disappointment of relegation from the top flight, the heartache of play-off defeat and sadness at leaving their beloved old Den in 1993. Hopes had been raised and dashed and the spectre of sanctions hung over their head. All this had now passed.

The new place was starting to feel like home and it felt as though the skies above The Den had finally cleared. Lions fans were ready to celebrate. Surely *this* would be their year?

Millwall fans were right to prepare themselves for excitement. The 1995/96 season would be a Millwall season like no other...

Endsleigh League Division One 1994-95 Final Table

Middlesbrough	**46**	**23**	**13**	**10**	**67**	**40**	**+27**	**82**	**Champions**
Reading	**46**	**23**	**10**	**13**	**58**	**44**	**+14**	**79**	
Bolton Wanderers	**46**	**21**	**14**	**11**	**67**	**45**	**+22**	**77**	**Play-off winners**
Wolves	**46**	**21**	**13**	**12**	**77**	**61**	**+16**	**76**	
Tranmere Rovers	**46**	**22**	**10**	**14**	**67**	**58**	**+9**	**76**	
Barnsley	46	20	12	14	63	52	+11	72	
Watford	46	19	13	14	52	46	+6	70	
Sheffield United	46	17	17	12	74	55	+19	68	
Derby County	46	18	12	16	66	51	+15	66	
Grimsby Town	46	17	14	15	62	56	+6	65	
Stoke City	46	16	15	15	50	53	-3	63	
Millwall	46	16	14	16	60	60	0	62	
Southend United	46	18	8	20	54	73	-19	62	
Oldham Athletic	46	16	13	17	60	60	0	61	
Charlton Athletic	46	16	11	19	58	66	-8	59	
Luton Town	46	15	13	18	61	64	-3	58	
Port Vale	46	15	13	18	58	64	-6	58	
Portsmouth	46	15	13	18	53	63	-10	58	
WBA	46	16	10	20	51	57	-6	58	
Sunderland	46	12	18	16	41	45	-4	54	
Swindon Town	**46**	**12**	**12**	**22**	**54**	**73**	**-19**	**48**	**Relegated**
Burnley	**46**	**11**	**13**	**22**	**49**	**74**	**-25**	**46**	**Relegated**
Bristol City	**46**	**11**	**12**	**23**	**42**	**63**	**-21**	**45**	**Relegated**
Notts County	**46**	**9**	**13**	**24**	**45**	**66**	**-21**	**40**	**Relegated**

To be continued...

Also by the author:

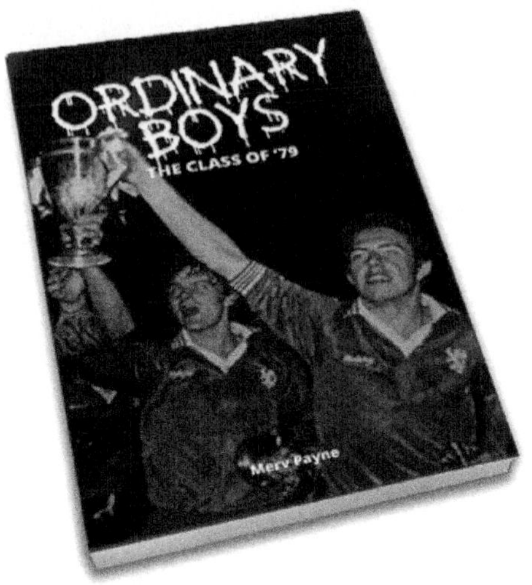

They were just a bunch of ordinary football-mad boys from the local estates, but together on the football pitch they were unstoppable.

This is the story of the Millwall team that won the FA Youth Cup for the first time in the club's history in 1979, but they were so much more than just a team.

An inseparable band of brothers, they defied the odds by not only beating some of the top teams in the country on their way to the final, they out-footballed them.

What was all the more remarkable was that they did it while the football club imploded around them under a constant wave of financial and other off-the-field troubles as it plummeted towards lower league footballing oblivion.

The club's dwindling fortunes would surely be turned around with the help of this new crop of brilliant young players graduating to the team.

Unfortunately, as we know, football isn't always quite as simple as that.

August 1988. The second Summer of Love. The UK wasn't basking in a heatwave, but the euphoric mix of acid house, rave and psychedelia meant that most were completely oblivious to the weather anyway. A year that had started like any other had blossomed in a feel good factor not experienced since the sixties. Love was in the air, house prices were up, unemployment was down and Millwall were in the First Division...

The Lions' appearance at football's top table for the first time in their 103 year history is probably best compared with Punk than Rave culture. Exploding on the scene and sticking two fingers up to the establishment, shocking their way to the top of the pile before being chewed up and spat out and then disappearing as quickly as they had arrived. But this was 1988 not 1976 and while their somewhat unwelcome arrival was no less dramatic and explosive than the opening chords to Anarchy in The UK, there was little bit more class about these boys as they slotted into the high life to the assured but no less revolutionary backing track of Voodoo Ray.

This is the story of a humble south London football club and its unique fans. How a team, built on a shoestring budget and made up largely of locals and boyhood Millwall supporters stunned the football world for a brief but beautiful time back in 1988 when football really was the beautiful game. For two years Millwall rubbed shoulders with the game's elite. Their fans, when they weren't raving in fields or warehouses, were gleefully gatecrashing a party where only the wealthy usually received an invite. There was delight and disappointment, triumph and tragedy, but what a ride.

During the late eighties, the drug of choice was Ecstasy, but for many, just following Millwall was enough, a truly natural high. With contributions from members of that historic Millwall squad as well as fans and opposition players and fans, this is a footballing tale that will never be repeated. Enjoy this trip, and it is a trip...

Also by the author:

Merv was determined to forge a bond with his dad. It's usually the other way around, but he could tell from a very young age that he'd probably have to do most of the work himself.

After going to their first football match together when he was seven, a shared passion began that would last the rest of their lives - which is just as well, because they had very little else to cement their bond.

Merv's attempts to enhance this relationship through junior football almost had disastrous consequences, but their passion for football – and in particular Millwall – became the glue that held them together.

What Merv really wanted was to share unique, unprecedented success at Millwall with his dad – something that was very thin on the ground in the early eighties. What they both wanted more than anything was to see their team in the First Division for the first time.

Because My Dad Does is a nostalgic journey through the days of the terraces, following your team - with and without your dad - on teletext or the football special, and sharing a once-in-a-lifetime, never-to-be-repeated football season as father and son.

All titles available now in paperback or Kindle format at

amazon

Or buy online at:

www.afterthelordmayorsshow.co.uk

Victor
PUBLISHING
victorpublishing.co.uk

Printed in Great Britain
by Amazon